habits

of

freedom

"For most of my life, I thought that indifference was a bad thing. When I ran across the Ignatian concept of 'holy indifference,' however, my eyes were opened in a new way. I learned of the peace that comes from accepting God's will in all things. It was a life-changing revelation. In *Habits of Freedom*, Fr. Christopher Collins does a great job presenting the teachings of St. Ignatius of Loyola to a new generation. I'm grateful for this book and I'll benefit from it for years to come. I know you will too!"

Gary Zimak
Author of *Give Up Worry for Lent!*

"If you are seeking ways to hear God's voice in the busyness, *Habits of Freedom* is the book for you. Weaving storytelling, practical advice, and exercises for prayer, Fr. Collins breaks down St. Ignatius's discernment wisdom in a relatable and easily digestible way. This is a book I will be sharing with the people I accompany in spiritual direction!"

Becky Eldredge
Spiritual director, retreat facilitator, and author

"St. Ignatius's writings on the Principle and Foundation, the Examen, and especially on the Rules for Discernment are rich and profound but not always easy to understand and apply. *Habits of Freedom* cracks the code, teasing out the ways these sixteenth-century texts can guide us today."

Mark E. Thibodeaux, SJ
Author of *Going Deeper*

habits

of

freedom

5 Ignatian Tools
for Clearing Your Mind
and Resting Daily
in the Lord

CHRISTOPHER S. COLLINS, SJ

AVE MARIA PRESS AVE Notre Dame, Indiana

© 2022 by Christopher S. Collins

Founded in 1865, Ave Maria Press is a ministry of the United States Province of Holy Cross.

www.avemariapress.com

Paperback: ISBN-13 978-1-64680-123-7

E-book: ISBN-13 978-1-64680-124-4

Cover image © Sven Hagolani / Getty Images.

Cover and text design by Brianna Dombo.

Printed and bound in the United States of America.

Library of Congress Cataloging-in-Publication Data is available.

Contents

Introduction

Discerning a Way Forward

As I sit down to write this introduction, it is almost exactly one year since the coronavirus outbreak was declared a pandemic. At that time, Saint Louis University, where I had been working, sent all students, faculty, and staff home. About eighteen Jesuits in our community of nearly ninety moved out almost overnight to reduce the risk we brought to our older brothers. We moved again a few months later within St. Louis. I moved a third time for a sabbatical at Boston College and then relocated to the Twin Cities to begin working at my alma mater, the University of St. Thomas. I hope that's it for the moving for a while!

For myself at least, the early days of the pandemic were characterized not so much by fear of getting sick, but rather by a slow-rolling wave of confusion and disorientation and a blur of days. The rapid changes in my living situation and uncertainty about my next mission as a Jesuit added to the blur. There was a fogginess in my ability to see the reality in front of me. Almost everything in my immediate sphere had been slowed down drastically. This was a sharp contrast to the frenetic pace of exciting work I had been a part of right up to the time of the lockdowns. In hindsight, I realize that the situation of the pandemic could have afforded me a time for deep reflection, contemplation, and spiritual renewal. I was hoping that might be the case. If I'm honest, though, I must say that it was a struggle.

Over the course of those months, I certainly experienced moments of beauty and joy, but it was a time marked far more by fogginess and instability. It was hard to fully engage with much. The future was uncertain for all of us, I suppose, but I'll speak for myself. I didn't know where I would be living. I didn't know exactly what my next work would be, though I figured it would be in some university setting. I didn't know what the future would hold for colleges and universities, which have been the context of my work for the better part of the last twenty years. Economic uncertainty for so many loomed large.

It might all still bounce back to "normal," whatever that is, but that now seems less and less likely. We have experienced massive shifts socially, economically, politically, and religiously. I don't think any of us knows how things are going to play out. But this sense of instability and uncertainty might always be reality. The pandemic only made these characteristics of the reality we always live in so much more immediate and poignant. The challenge, then, is posed anew: how to sort out what's going on in the world and in my own mind and heart in the midst of this uncertainty and instability. And how is God present in all of it? In other words, how do we best discern a way forward?

Discernment

I've learned about and talked about discernment of spirits quite a bit over the years. But making the effort to say something useful and hopefully clear in the middle of the fog of the pandemic was challenging. It's ironic on many levels to have been asked to write a book on discernment of spirits at a time when I was not doing that discerning very well myself!

But it's a practice nonetheless that stands out as essential now more than ever. Discerning how to proceed with life—not just with big decisions, but with more immediate habits of daily living—is crucial if we want to stay on track. To be happy. To be free. To be free enough to love and to live fully.

"Discernment" is often meant to denote the act of trying to make a decision in a thoughtful, prudent manner. Typically, it is reserved for major life decisions including what a person's vocation is, who to marry, what profession to choose, what to major in in college, and so on. An abundance of materials and techniques are available to aid in these pivotal life choices.

In the Christian tradition, discernment takes on a slightly more distinctive meaning. It is a practice undertaken not as an individual person but in relation with and inspired by the Holy Spirit. It is a way of discovering pathways that lead to greater love, to full flourishing as a person in community, and to greater freedom to live out one's vocation to love and to serve. It is a practice rooted in relationship (with the God who *is* a set of relationships) and oriented toward relationships, toward freedom and the love that freedom makes possible.

There is also a more focused tradition of discernment stemming from the contributions of St. Ignatius of Loyola, the founder of the Jesuits. This tradition offers tools not only for making big life decisions but also for cultivating habits of daily living. These tools help us pay attention to how the Holy Spirit and the evil spirit impact us in our struggle to remain free and able to live full, happy, and generous lives as we all desire.

St. Ignatius and the
Discernment of Spirits

In 1521, St. Ignatius was wounded in battle at Pamplona in Spain. He was a soldier in service to the king and was trying (foolishly, as it turns out) to defend a fortress that was being attacked by the French. Out of the trauma of being wounded came a great conversion of heart for Ignatius and a total transformation of a "young man given to the vanities of the world," as he described himself. Exactly five centuries ago, that process of conversion began to unfold for Ignatius of Loyola. He moved into a cave at Manresa, not far from Barcelona, near the Cardoner River and in the shadow of the ancient Benedictine monastery Montserrat. There, in that cave and while visiting the monks and walking along the river, he slowly allowed himself to be transformed by the inner promptings of the Holy Spirit. The Good Spirit led him deeper and deeper to a true sense of himself, a true sense of how God saw him. The Good Spirit also led him to a true sense of confidence in the gifts that had been given to him to give glory to God by spending himself for the good of his neighbor.

But while in that cave, Ignatius also learned how the evil one—the enemy of our true human nature, as he referred to Satan—operated in his life and in the lives of all of us. He learned the methods of the enemy, who always aims at leading us into separation from God, others, and ourselves, leaving us in isolation, loneliness, and discouragement. In other words, Ignatius learned that there are forces both within and without us that can obscure our ability to see who we truly are, who God truly is, and what the world really looks like in light of the providence, or care, of God. We can be hindered in our ability to see and therefore to act in true freedom and out of love. After much prayer, a variety of interior experiences, reflection on those experiences, and spiritual conversation with the Benedictine monks at Montserrat, Ignatius started to make notes about what he was learning. He learned how the Holy Spirit was moving him in the direction of greater faith, hope, and love—what he called the experience of "consolation." At the same time, he learned how the evil spirit was leading him in the opposite direction, into discouragement, fear, and anxiety—what he called "desolation."

Many would say the greatest gift Ignatius left to the Church was the set of rules that he laid out for people as aids to distinguish how the evil spirit (the enemy) works on us and how the Holy Spirit simultaneously does so. Below is a brief description of some of the first set of rules, or guidelines, that Ignatius offers. These are not all of the rules, but they are, in my estimation, the most basic ones to be attentive to for the purpose of our daily quest to remain free, happy, and loving. I have put the rules in my own language.

Basic Rules for Discernment of Spirits

Ignatius describes the nature of these guidelines as follows: "Rules to aid us toward perceiving and then understanding, at least to some extent, the various motions which are caused in the soul: the good motions that they may be received and the bad that they be rejected" (*Spiritual Exercises* #313).

1. For a person moving away from God, from one mortal sin to another, the enemy proposes pleasures meant to attach the person to sin, which is a state of separation from God. For this person, the Holy Spirit produces a sting of conscience to free them from those attachments. (#314)

2. For the person basically oriented toward union with God and pursuing the good life, the enemy instigates anxiety to sadden and to unsettle the person by false reasons aimed at preventing progress. In this context, the Good Spirit stirs up courage, consolations, tears, inspirations, and tranquility. (Doing a daily examen confirms these movements.) (#315)

3. Remember the nature of consolation: motion in the soul through which one is stirred to love of Creator and Lord (humility); tears; increase in faith, hope, and love; attraction to heavenly, eternal goods that produce deep happiness and peace. (#316)

4. Remember the nature of desolation: obtuseness of soul and turmoil within it; impulsive motion toward low and earthly things; feelings of listlessness, tepidity, unhappiness, separation from God. (#317)

5. Never make a change while in a state of desolation. By following counsels of the evil one, we can never find a way to a right decision. (#318)

6. A person feeling stuck in desolation should follow the principle of *agere contra*—"go against." This is the admonition to go against natural inclinations or habits that are producing attachments that limit freedom. (#319)

7. Be patient in desolation. Consolation will return. (#321)

Overview

In the reflections that follow in this book, I hope to provide a framework for how to take advantage of these insights of St. Ignatius in an ordinary, everyday manner. It is my hope that this framework might help you (and me!) stay grounded in the peace and confidence that come from being constantly confirmed in the love that God has for each of us.

But this is not just a private matter. What I propose should never lead to the kind of introspection that causes self-preoccupation. These are not merely a series of self-help techniques. Hopefully what follows will help lead us beyond ourselves as we move through this life, in faith and in hope and in love of God and those around us. Woven between the lessons are reflections on particularly evocative scriptural passages as well as some personal stories. My hope is that these offerings can be prompts to spark your own memories and imagination to see how your life has been and is always unfolding within the one world of God's grace that we all inhabit.

Whether you're on the cusp of making a major life decision or you're simply seeking peace in your day-to-day, this book seeks to encourage you in:

- Establishing some imaginative frameworks for how to interpret what goes on in your daily life;
- Paying attention to your moods and perceptions of reality;
- Resisting negative influences;
- Developing spiritual and emotional growth and resiliency; and
- Combating discouragement, resentment, and fear so that you can live more freely and generously.

In the first chapter I offer some basic considerations that might help us to be disposed to do the work of discernment of spirits. The first consideration has to do with the uncomfortable reality of being *displaced* or *destabilized* in order to be free to discern. In "The First Principle and Foundation" of the *Spiritual Exercises*, Ignatius indicates how important it is that we try to remain "indifferent" to the aspects of life that we so easily get attached to. Indifference in this sense is not apathy, but rather a disposition of being free of any "disordered attachments." Sometimes it is precisely when we are thrown off balance, when things don't go our way, when we lose control, that we are most opened up to the possibility of being free enough to see a deeper vision and have the ability to make choices that will more fully lead us where we want to go.

In the next two chapters, I reflect on the importance of *remembering the basic narrative*, the basic truths of our lives, and, conversely, of *rejecting the lies* we sometimes believe that cause us to forget who we are in God's sight. The goal here is to continually practice the act of remembering, grasping, and reconfirming the *identity* that God has given us from the very beginning and also to continually root out the distortions that obscure our ability to see this truth and live out of it on a daily basis.

With those considerations in place, the final two chapters get into some tactical helps for us along the way. First, since discernment never occurs in isolation, but always in the context of friendship with God, the way forward involves constant communication with God. *Dialogue in prayer*, and also in the setting of spiritual conversation with a friend who is also trying to live in friendship with God, is crucial. We simply cannot find the way to freedom and happiness in isolation and by thinking thoughts in our own heads. If we are talking to ourselves, we will surely get disoriented and ultimately paralyzed, unable to find a way forward. In dialogue, perspective begins to emerge. And this dialogue must be ongoing.

Finally, discernment cannot be undertaken in a vacuum. It is not ultimately the territory of abstraction, thought, or even just prayer alone. *Action* is necessary. Living is necessary. Doing concrete things with other in-the-flesh human persons is the stuff of real discernment! In this sense, the final principle I would suggest leads us back to where we started—paying attention to real-life experience, to our lived histories. And then the process starts over again as we continue that pathway toward building habits of freedom on a daily basis.

1

Allow Disruption

"Can these bones come back to life?"
Ezekiel 37:3

Seeking in the Desert

Throughout the scriptures, people come to understand who they are in relationship with God through the central image of the desert. The desert, as terrifying as it might be, can also be precisely the place of discovery of the true self. The fundamental narrative of the Old Testament, for example, is that of the Exodus. When the people of God wander far away and find themselves stuck in slavery, God hears their cry and leads them back to union with himself, back home. But the way back is through the desert. They must be led through the place of greatest insecurity, where they cannot provide for themselves but must be taken care of every day, at every moment, by the God who loves them, feeds them, and tends to them. If they try to store up resources for themselves and begin to not rely on God anymore, it does not go well. God gives them enough to eat every day in the desert by providing manna from heaven. But it is only enough for the day. The Israelites begin to grumble under these conditions. They long to go back into slavery, where they at least felt more at ease and in familiar circumstances. But God continues to lead them on, in friendship with himself.

Pope Benedict XVI, in one of his writings about the worship of God that liberates his people, makes a fascinating, if troubling, observation. He notes that during the Exodus, the word of God comes to the people indicating that he wants to lead them out into the desert *so that* they can properly worship him, to be in union with him. Seen in this light, the desert is not so much a necessary evil to get through, but exactly the place where God wants to meet his people, that they might enter into union with him, into true intimacy and friendship. In a sense, the desert is the destination itself. Only in the desert, when we have nothing to rely on of our own making or of our own doing, can we truly *find God* and therefore become our true selves, in reliance on God's care and friendship.

At another time when God's people had gotten themselves in a bind, the word of God comes to them through the prophet Hosea: "Yet it was I who taught Ephraim to walk, who took them in my arms; but they did not know that I cared for them. I drew them with human cords, with bands of love; I fostered them like those who raise an infant to their cheeks; I bent down to feed them" (11:3–4). To me, it's good to be reminded, in times when I'm not necessarily in crisis and in a fog of confusion, that this is what God is like. This tenderness that God has when looking upon his beloved ones drives how he wants to communicate with us. And he yearns for us to cooperate a little bit so that he can care for us in this way and draw close, through "human cords" and "bands of love." The desert, then, the place of what feels like alienation, can become a place of great tenderness and union with God, if we allow him to draw us close. Only if we give way to this intimacy will we begin to find our way back onto the path that leads us home, to freedom.

Vision on the Beach

I had one of these life-changing encounters, not in a desert, but on a beach. The summer after high school I lived, along with two other American high school kids, with a family in a very small village in the Andes Mountains in Ecuador. I applied for this program at the beginning of my senior year, not so much out of altruism, but frankly, for something different to do, for some adventure, and maybe as a way of making new friends. The decision to take part in this program would never have come about if things had not fallen apart pretty drastically for me.

A little bit of a context. My mom, dad, and I had moved in the middle of my junior year from Phoenix, Arizona, to Dallas, Texas. My older siblings were already out of the house, into college and beyond. So I was the only kid at home when my dad got a great new job in another state that was a way forward for him after conditions at his previous job had deteriorated. It wasn't just me; my whole family experienced being destabilized. For myself, though, I was totally upended. I was "taken away" from friends and an increasingly fun social scene—from driving around town with my new driver's license and going to parties (and getting grounded thanks to those parties!). I also was separated from a great girlfriend. A truly tragic romance! It felt like the end of the world. I wallowed heavily in self-pity during those first several months, and I'm sure I made everyone around me, especially my parents, miserable. I wanted to drag them into my misery as only a sixteen-year-old boy can do, I suppose. Anyway, it was awful all the way around.

In the midst of that cloud, however, I heard about a program where high school students could spend the summer volunteering in Latin America on a health project. That sounded exciting and at least something different, so I applied for it and was accepted. I probably had some noble hopes of wanting to help people as well, but mostly I saw it as a chance to meet new people, make some friends, and have an adventure. I was motivated, at least in part, by self-centeredness, looking back at it.

It was a bit of a rough start. Since I didn't know much Spanish, I was mostly smiling and nodding in our initial conversations with various families. Thank God the two girls I was with were much better at Spanish. So at first it was pretty jarring and disorienting. But along the way, I was drawn out of myself. In a new culture where I didn't know the language, in a rural setting where there was nothing to entertain myself (malls, TV, etc.) as well as no running water or electricity, I was feeling pretty vulnerable. But in the midst of those circumstances, I also began to feel happier than I ever remembered being up to that point. I was surprised. With everything stripped away—all the material goods, the comforts, the familiarity of life—I actually felt freer and more joyful. That summer shifted a lot inside of me.

When we were debriefing at the end of the summer on a beach outside Guayaquil, on the Pacific coast, I was sitting one evening with four or five friends who had just gone through the same experience. I recall looking out at the horizon over the ocean and thinking about what was coming up for me as I was about to start college in a couple weeks. Having just had my world pretty well rocked and thrown up for grabs, I felt like that future ahead, that vision before me, was infinitely wide open and uncertain. I knew that I had changed and had new desires, and what I had been planning for college and beyond was now all out the window. My thoughts about being an investment banker didn't resonate in the same way now. I had absolutely no idea what to expect, but somehow I knew in the deepest part of myself that whatever was ahead in my future was going to be great. And I had no control over it, apparently. I was wide open. Excited and petrified at the same time. And with all that moving around in my mind and heart, I started to bawl like a baby on that beach. I felt so raw, so helpless in a sense, so out of control. But I also felt so excited, so hopeful, and somehow so grateful and humbled by where I was at that moment. I felt small but also great, like I had a big future ahead of me. And in a very elusive and yet tangible way, what moved me most was the sense that somehow I was going to be most powerfully cared for and loved throughout it all. Only years later would I attribute that sense to God caring for me—with "human cords" and "bands of love," you might say.

A New Path

I think in many ways that moment on the beach is where my vocation to be a priest and a Jesuit started to take root. I wasn't particularly religious and certainly not prayerful at that time, but still, something overtook me inside that made me pay attention, that opened up my vision and a way of imagining my future. If I hadn't been decentered in so many ways prior to that, I doubt that I would have been disposed to discover that my path was going to somehow be about serving others and having the presence of God one way or another accompany me throughout the whole thing. Somehow the whole path, if I lived it well, would be taken care of, provided for, sustained. In hindsight, I would say that moment was one of the most

profound experiences of the care and providence of God that
I have had even though I did not have the language for it at
that time. I just knew that my life was going to be good and
exciting and that I couldn't wait to get after it!

On a very natural level, then, my life's circumstances
brought me into a place of vulnerability and a feeling of being
decentered, not in control. In that place, it became more possible for me to pay closer attention to the movements of my
own heart and soul. Because things had become destabilized,
I could begin to make some fundamental choices for my life
that would lead to greater freedom, greater life, and greater
joy as well as set aside some other options that would lead me
into self-centeredness and less happiness. Without knowing
it, I'd say God was using that experience to begin to teach me
about how to discern the various spirits operating on me that
I didn't know were active or even existed. Even more important, I received a glimpse of a big vision of what my life could
become.

*Maybe you'd like to take a moment now and think back on your
life and see if you have had some experience that really threw
you, but that ended up opening new possibilities for you. Maybe
speak with God a little bit about that history and thank him for
staying with you and opening up a new pathway for your life.*

"The First Principle and Foundation"

That experience in Ecuador helped me to let go of preconcep-
tions of what my life would be like and gave me a bigger vision
for the future with God leading the way. It was, in hindsight, a
lived experience of what St. Ignatius talked about five centuries

ago. "The First Principle and Foundation" I alluded to in the introduction is something like a preamble or an overture to the whole of the *Spiritual Exercises.* In that text, St. Ignatius gives a very big-picture perspective on the aim and purpose of our lives. We are created by God for the sake of union with God, ultimately. We are to praise, reverence, and serve God. Our ultimate happiness comes only in that union. In everyday life, then, our days are filled with countless particular possibilities and scenarios that, depending on how we respond to them, might draw us closer in that union with God or else move us farther away. That's why it is so important, Ignatius says, to try to keep a disposition of indifference about the things and the choices before us. The indifference we do well to practice is to be understood, not as apathy, but as an interior disposition that is unattached or unbiased ahead of time about which direction to go in with any particular choice.

Being in this state of "holy indifference" is important because life can surprise us. That is to say, the grace of God in the midst of life can surprise us. It is not uncommon that when things seem to fall apart, we actually come a lot closer to being opened up to the fullness of the grace of God in our lives. Ignatius goes on to explain that it is better not to prefer "wealth over poverty, health over sickness or a long life over a short one" because when life presents to us what is not most obviously desirable, new life can unfold in surprising ways. Out of suffering, loss, or uncertainty can come new realities in which we are drawn closer to God precisely because of circumstances that we would never have chosen for ourselves or for anyone else.

This ability of God to draw close and make his presence felt in the middle of difficult circumstances makes it all the more essential that we practice discernment. We need to be

able to tell the difference between how the Holy Spirit is leading us on toward union and true freedom, and how the evil
spirit is leading us away from God into fear, anxiety, and isolation, in the midst of those same uncertain circumstances. But
this ability to discern spirits takes practice. Lots of it. The good
thing is, every moment of our lives presents opportunities for
us to keep practicing and to keep on learning!

Finding or Seeking?

Perhaps the fundamental aspect of spirituality in the tradition of St. Ignatius of Loyola is the proposal that it is possible
to "find God in all things." But there is a bit of a controver-
sy about this motto even in Ignatian spirituality circles. Did
Ignatius say *find* God in all things or *seek* God in all things? I
felt a little energized when I was introduced into that debate.
Finding God seems pretty definitive, and it also seems a bit
of a tall order at times. But the admonition to *seek* God in all
things, in the ordinary, daily experiences of our own corner
of the world, strikes me as more realistic. *Seeking* suggests that
we may or may not be "successful" in that daily quest. Some
days might present more challenges than others. *Seeking* char-
acterizes the realism of the struggle that we often face to find
God when God can be hard to find.

Bishop Robert Barron, in *The Strangest Way*, a book that I
use when I teach college freshmen, talks about the pathway of
Christianity as one that must involve becoming decentered, or
destabilized, at times. Only when we experience being unsettled (which comes naturally enough with life, anyway) can
we be opened up in new and fresh ways to the grace of God
that comes with encounter with Jesus. Finding and encountering the presence of God can be challenging when our vision
so easily gets clouded. Especially when we have become

disoriented, been displaced in any number of ways—by losing a job, experiencing the death of a loved one, being significantly wounded in a relationship that we thought was a constant—we can be thrown off balance and begin to ask, Where is God? What is God doing here? How am I to respond? In these times of being displaced or decentered, our *seeking* for God becomes not just a nice, pious thing to do but an urgent necessity.

This striving to find, this seeking, is imperative for us on a daily basis. It is not easy all the time. In fact, that's why Ignatius encourages us to cultivate habits of seeking. He says it will be work. These are *exercises* to be undertaken, and exercise, at least for me, does not come easy! But the more we exercise, the better shape we get into. Or at least so I've heard. I am no model of fitness at the present moment, physical, spiritual, or otherwise! And yet we always have another chance to begin to cultivate these habits. When things fall apart a bit, when I lose my center and my way, it is then that I not only need help to get back on track, but also especially want to know that I am not alone. That I have a friend. A companion on the way in a tumultuous time.

Going to the Desert Daily

When we speak of discernment of spirits, we are talking about an ongoing process. It is not a one-and-done thing. In fact, the Latin root of the word "discernment" means "to separate out, to distinguish." This implies a multiplicity of things before us, and we need to sort out what's what. Separate out the good from the bad. Separate out what is most authentic from what is less so. Separate out truest, deepest desires from more superficial ones. Separate out truth from the deceptions that we sometimes fall for.

My experience in Ecuador and subsequent reflection on that experience on the beach was a major grace in my life, and it happened without me doing much to help it along. It was *given*. But I did make a choice to go somewhere that was uncertain for an extended period and tried to be open to what would happen. In that sense, I was disposed to receive such a powerful grace. And that's been a good reminder for me ever since. Putting myself into unknown, uncertain, some- what insecure circumstances has a way of disposing me to receive something greater than I could have expected. That has been the case for me in my vocation as a priest and as a Jesuit. Taking vows of poverty, chastity, and obedience, trying to fundamentally say yes to that call and commit to a way of life that is inherently insecure and decentered, has afforded me countless opportunities to experience new things, meet new people, and be drawn into new works that I never would have discovered otherwise. I don't live this life well every day, but fundamentally, I'm grateful I've said yes to this invitation from God to dispose myself to be opened up to what is greater than myself.

That same kind of grace can be given on a daily basis in less dramatic and yet very important ways related to our desire for happiness. There is a deception that can take over in our daily lives, in the midst of our busyness and all the responsi- bilities of work, family, household affairs, and so on. We can come under the illusion that we are running all of these things. We are in charge. We are in control. We might fail at times, but still, we are the ones really taking care of business! But in my own life I have learned that when I take time to step back, to detach a bit and reflect on what went on in the day, I get the sense that yes, I was active, but so were a lot of other things. A lot of life happened without me being at the center of it. I'm living in a much bigger world than that of my own creation. That daily recognition can be either unsettling—to come face to face with the fact that I am not in control—or refreshing and liberating. Gaining some perspective like this and getting the focus off myself can be a great gift. In kind of a nice way, when I pause and take in the larger picture of all that has been going on, I can feel *small* for a little while and have a sense of wonder instead of anxiety, especially if I step back and look at things not through the lens of my own responsibilities and duties, but through the lens of God laboring to make his love known in the little things on a daily basis.

The Examen

Ignatius's admonition to Jesuits under his care that they must commit daily (even twice daily) to an examen is well known. Stepping back, spending time in quiet and reflection, and paying attention to the movements of the spirits bears much fruit and helps sensitize us to where there is life and where the pitfalls are. Being attuned to the presence of God in the small things and also taking time to uncover and reject the movements of the evil spirit are crucial to the possibility of staying on track, of seeking and finding God in all things, and of remaining free, unattached, and able to live and love as God created us—for happiness.

Just about every Jesuit I know (myself included) grasps how important this focused prayer, this paying attention, is. Yet almost all of us also struggle with being faithful to it. I'm not sure why that is, but it's common. Maybe we just get busy with many things, and pausing in the middle of all our daily responsibilities is hard to do. Perhaps it feels like it's not productive. Anyway, it's common.

The benefit of the examen, however, came much more to the fore for me recently. When the lockdown of the coronavirus pandemic hit, our small staff at the university where I worked quickly tried to figure out how to adapt. In regular times we were charged with being a pastoral presence for faculty, staff, and to some degree alumni, and we felt that responsibility in a new way. We discussed how to stay in touch with people, to provide support, some sense of community, and encouragement in the midst of having been sent home to isolate for the foreseeable future. We had already built up a small virtual community through Facebook, which we had mostly used to invite people to events that we sponsored. With that network in place, we now committed to take turns among ourselves to lead a very brief examen every day at noon. People could join in, in real time, to do the examen together. It was a very consoling moment of community to be joined like that. A strange community, but a community nevertheless. And in my experience, there was a certain intensity about those few moments on a daily basis. As one day began to blur into the next during that time, many of us struggled to remain encouraged, grateful, and fully alive. The particularities of life that make every day stand out as beautiful and worth living became harder and harder to see. But this simple practice, undertaken every day, allowed the reality of God's presence and the uniqueness of that day to shine through for a few moments. And when that light shines through, we are given what is necessary to keep on moving through the day with grace and confidence.

The Living Word of God

So, on a very natural level of human experience, against the backdrop of being in an unsettled or decentered place, the

Holy Spirit can and does move our human hearts toward freedom and union with God, with others, and with ourselves. In
this sense, God can be found in the ordinary circumstances
of life and sometimes in quite surprising ways. But ultimately,
the clearest and most reliable pathway to this freedom and
union with God lies in encountering him through his own
Word communicated in scripture. This Word is itself "living
and effective, sharper than any two-edged sword, penetrating
even between soul and spirit, joints and marrow, and able to
discern reflections and thoughts of the heart" (Heb 4:12).

On a natural level, then, we can dispose ourselves to an
encounter with God, and then, even further, in a supernatural
way, we can enter into that encounter by listening with the ears
of the heart to what God wants to say to us. In the next chapters of this book, I will contemplate with you a few of those
words of God that, though ancient, still have the potential
of moving us in the present and into that saving and loving
encounter with God. For the moment, though, I'd like to focus
on one vivid image from scripture that spoke to me recently in
light of the circumstances in which I undertook this writing
in the midst of the isolation of the pandemic.

This scripture, which came around in the cycle of daily
readings for the liturgy, hit me rather viscerally. I had been
struggling, as I think many had been, with the lack of human,
in-the-flesh, social interaction and concrete work to be done
with others to address concrete needs in the world. Being constantly masked in public and being relegated largely to Zoom
meetings had taken a toll. I had the feeling of being untethered, ungrounded, maybe even a little unhinged at times, from
the life I had previously known as "normal." Living in the present moment in such a fog made it hard to find energy and to
muster creativity.

Against this backdrop, I read the readings for the day and my heart leapt. It was that striking image from the book of the prophet Ezekiel. In the context of the exile of the people of Israel, God speaks through his prophet, urging him to prophesy to the people who had become lost, alienated, and untethered in their exile. Into a wasteland of death and decay, God speaks words of new creation:

> The hand of the LORD came upon me, and he led me out in the spirit of the LORD and set me in the center of the broad valley. It was filled with bones. He made me walk among them in every direction. So many lay on the surface of the valley! How dry they were! He asked me: Son of man, can these bones come back to life? "LORD GOD," I answered, "you alone know that." Then he said to me: Prophesy over these bones, and say to them: Dry bones, hear the word of the LORD! Thus says the LORD GOD to these bones: Listen! I will make breath enter you so you may come to life. I will put sinews on you, make flesh grow over you, cover you with skin, and put breath into you so you may come to life. Then you shall know that I am the LORD. I prophesied as I had been commanded. A sound started up, as I was prophesying, rattling like thunder. The bones came together, bone joining to bone. As I watched, sinews appeared on them, flesh grew over them, skin covered them on top, but there was no breath in them. Then he said to me: Prophesy to the breath, prophesy, son of man! Say to the breath: Thus says the LORD GOD: From the four winds come, O breath, and breathe into these slain that they may come to life. I prophesied as he commanded me, and the breath entered them; they came to life and stood on their feet, a

> vast army. He said to me: Son of man, these bones
> are the whole house of Israel!" (Ez 37:1–11)

In the unfolding of this scene, God sees his people lost, decaying, and dying. He makes a promise that he will bring them back to life, give them fresh hearts, and bring them home. He fulfills that promise through the prophet Ezekiel, who "prophesies," that is, speaks directly those words of God to the dry bones and watches them come back to life with flesh, with sinew, and then ultimately with a breath of spirit to enliven them.

This dramatic, unfolding process spoke to my heart so poignantly when I read it. It is important to note that this was a familiar passage to me and one that I've been captivated by before. But in times of isolation and fogginess and untetheredness, the vision struck me as new, as fresh, and as GOOD news. I wanted it to be true. And I was convinced that God desires it also. That vision of new life being brought to old, dry bones became a source of new encouragement for me. My own disposition plus the content of the Word itself combined for something special to happen. New life and new hope crept into me. I still need to revisit that vision and look for ways to allow myself to be transformed and to cooperate with that vision, but it was a new beginning.

And so it is, no matter what our current circumstances are. It is essential to pay attention to where we are right now, to acknowledge what we're feeling right now, to articulate the way we see the world right now. And then to open up. Allow ourselves to be displaced, decentered. To be opened up to something different. And then to allow the Holy Spirit to move, to act, to allow the Word of God to be spoken and heard by me, by us.

Exercises to Cultivate
Habits of Freedom

1. Unplugged exercise: Take twenty minutes to be still with nothing to distract you. Sit on a park bench. Recline in a chair. Lie in the backyard. Then jot down some notes about what came up in your thoughts and feelings. Was there gratitude? Peace? Anxiety? Worry? Regret? Anger? Chat with God about those reactions in an open-ended way.

2. Think about two times in life, one early and one more recent, when you have been decentered, or lost control. Recall the memory and let those feelings come back to you and sit with them for a bit. Allow yourself to feel raw or vulnerable. Was there any fruit that came out of those experiences?

3. Reflect upon an important relationship or aspect of your life that came about as a result of things falling apart or not going your way. Talk to God about that gift and spend some time thanking him for it.

2

Remember Who I Am and Whose I Am

"You are my Beloved. In you I am well pleased."
Mark 1:11

In these moments of being thrown off balance and even into a bit of a tailspin, we can lose our bearings. We can forget who we really are, and we can only know who we truly are when we are gazed upon through God's eyes. We can forget that we are "fearfully and wonderfully made" (Ps 139:14, NASB) and seen by him as the "apple of his eye" (Dt 32:10). The challenge of remembering this fundamental truth struck me a while back when I was recalling a couple of distinct memories from my days growing up. I remember driving around town with my mom. I think we had just gone to a drive-through for burgers. I was maybe seven or eight years old. We must have just come from Mass because I wanted to talk about that line we used to say right before Communion, "Lord, I am not worthy to receive you, but only say the word and I shall be healed." I was confused and more than a bit incensed, if a third-grader can be incensed. "Not worthy? I don't get it," I protested to my mom. "I'm not, *not worthy*! I'm very worthy. I'm a good kid. Everybody loves me. I don't see any reason why God wouldn't love me. What is this 'not worthy' business?! What kind of misstatements are we making in Mass? They ought to change that line!" I had great clarity.

I thought of that conversation in light of my college experience over a decade later. I remember going to the Sunday-night student Mass pretty much every week. The statement "I am not worthy to receive you, but only say the word and I shall be healed" now, funny enough, felt like the absolute perfect thing to be saying before getting in that Communion line. I was often a little worn out on Sunday evenings. The Friday and Saturday nights that preceded Sunday were usually lots of fun. Maybe too much fun. Perhaps I had not been making the best choices over the course of the weekend. The more I became aware of my sinfulness, my selfishness, the more it made sense to me to admit to being not worthy to receive the Lord. But I also had an increasing sense of wonder that he kept inviting me back and giving himself to me in the Eucharist. He stayed open to me and kept calling me back. Why would he do that? I am not worthy. All of a sudden, at a very different stage in life and under different circumstances, that line became my favorite in the whole Mass. It summed it all up: my need for God and his desire to give himself to me. Again and again. Exactly when I was not worthy.

This was a pretty significant moment in the discovery of my own vocation. I was in between. I had experience of the truth of being loved and belonging early on. Now I had the experience of not being worthy of that love. And yet the Lord kept inviting me to come close and let that love take over. But this was and is an ongoing unfolding. It is a journey, as they say. There are twists and turns. Some steps forward, some back. And yet the constant is God's fidelity and invitation. He keeps hoping that I will "get it" . . . don't forget it!

My Story Is Jesus's Story

In our attempts to make sense of the twists and turns of life, it helps to situate our own experiences into the one story of Jesus. God became one of us precisely so that he could share in our own human experience and redeem us from within that human experience. He also became one of us so we can know that God understands what we go through and that we are not alone. Because of the Incarnation, we know definitively that God is united to us by way of the Person of Jesus, in all that we go through. That might be pretty tough, maybe even impossible, to grasp theologically and philosophically. But at the very least, the life and story of Jesus provide us with an imaginative framework for every one of our lives, individually as well as collectively. We can find our life experiences *within* the story of Jesus's own life.

Specifically, I'd like to set up an imaginative framework for our own lives by considering the baptism of Jesus. This event comes after his time growing up in the relative solitude of Nazareth but before he begins his public ministry. It is a moment in his own life of being displaced from family and friends. He has left home. He's moved away from his mom. Presumably Joseph has already died. Jesus has no disciples yet. He's left his friends back home. There is no indication of having a place to move into. He doesn't seem to have a job, a source of income, a plan for the next steps in his life. As far as I can tell from the gospels, Jesus had nothing obvious in that moment to rely on for security. He is displaced and on the brink of something very big. Nothing short of the redemption of humanity, actually! But in that moment, he's got nothing to hold on to except one thing—the love that his eternal Father has for him, and the encouragement and guidance of the Holy Spirit. That's true not only for Jesus, but for ourselves as well. More on this later.

Discerning spirits has to do with reestablishing our freedom so that we can love the way we want to and that God hopes for us. We cannot be truly happy until we are truly free, and we need to know who it is that we truly are if we are to be truly free. The fundamental question, then, is, what is our true identity? This question is as fundamental as it gets. We see an answer illuminated most simply and perfectly in the story of Jesus's own baptism. But before delving further into that, let's look at a story, an imaginative framework for our consideration, that is a precursor to the story of Jesus and just as foundational for us.

In the Beginning

Let's listen to what God says about who we are and what our true identity is, and then let that truth of our identity shape our mission and activities. The very beginning of the Bible, the book of Genesis, reveals that we are creatures lovingly and deliberately created in the image and likeness of God. I would like to say, "The End," at this point. It's all we need to know, really. If we could live according to this truth, there would be no struggle. There would be no need for a book on discernment of spirits! The problem is that we forget. We forget who we are. We come to believe distortions of who we are. We believe lies and half-truths. And we forget, not only occasionally, but fundamentally and perpetually. Part of what it means to be human since the Fall in the garden of Eden has been that fundamental and perpetual forgetting.

The story is familiar, but let's revisit it briefly. After the first two creation stories in Genesis, everything is perfectly set up for Adam and Eve to do nothing but enjoy their lives. Enjoy the garden. Enjoy each other and their friendship with God. Everything that has been given has been given as gift, and the only thing to do for the greatest of those gifts, man and woman, is to receive and to enjoy. They don't need to work. They don't need to prove their worthiness of these gifts. They don't need to compete. Just receive and enjoy. Live in the present moment, receive, and enjoy.

But the present moment doesn't last too long. That day when a voice ever so subtly inserted itself, Eve and Adam slipped out of the present moment and started to fall for an appealing conversation that called things into question. They fell for an abstraction and a distorted promise for the future:

> Now the snake was the most cunning of all the wild animals that the LORD God had made. He asked the woman, "Did God really say, 'You shall not eat from any of the trees in the garden'?" The woman answered the snake: "We may eat of the fruit of the trees in the garden; it is only about the fruit of the tree in the middle of the garden that God said, 'You shall not eat it or even touch it, or else you will die.'" But the snake said to the woman: "You certainly will not die! God knows well that when you eat of it your eyes will be opened and you will be like gods, who know good and evil." (Gn 3:1–5)

The first thing the evil one does is to engage in a "what if" conversation. Disingenuously, the serpent starts with an exaggerated question: Did God really say, no fruit? Eve, with all piety and affection, defends God right away, saying, "No, he only said that about the one tree!" The problem is, by this time, Eve has already been hooked into a distorted conversation with a voice that is not that of God. She is now listening to and speaking with one who is not the One who created her out of love and who delights in her and desires the best for her. She is now speaking with the great deceiver and manipulator. She is also engaging in a dialogue grounded in not the present concrete reality but rather one of speculation. I think this is very telling and a great challenge to me personally. I love speculation. I love abstraction. I was a philosophy major! But I have also come to realize how often these abstractions lead down a dead-end path and ultimately to discouragement.

To put it more pointedly, when I fall into the trap of thinking thoughts to myself, of talking to myself, of playing out worst-case scenarios in the future or asking myself what if I hadn't made that mistake in the past, I consistently fall into discouragement, regret, shame, and fear. I become paralyzed. And I have slowly forgotten about God's presence with me right now, moment by moment. That's another telling aspect of the story in the garden. For a split second, in that one encounter with the serpent, Eve and later Adam are outside the presence of God and not talking to God directly. They start theorizing about what God said or didn't say. About what God might have been up to by placing this one tree off limits. What was he holding back from us? We thought he was good by giving us everything, including each other. But maybe not. Maybe he was being stingy. Maybe he didn't want us to have knowledge that would lead us to "be like gods"!

The strange thing about this story is that only a few verses earlier, God himself says, "Let us make human beings in our image, after our *likeness*" (Gn 1:26). *Likeness*. They are already *like God* from the very beginning. That's the way God made them. How did they forget? Adam and Eve already possessed a dignity and a destiny that was immense. It was filled with possibility and with purpose that they could not even conceive of. As long as they were in friendship with God and in daily conversation with him, the conditions were set such that they could live lives of infinite meaning, of purpose, of freedom, and of love. But that simple, discrete moment of forgetting changes everything in the story. All of a sudden, the vision shrinks. Fear, worry, and anxiety creep in. They start to operate out of a mentality of scarcity. It's a very sad twist to the story of Adam and Eve. But it's also sad because it says a lot about what our human condition is really like and how each one of us so easily falls into the same trap.

Forgetting, one might say, is our biggest problem. What if Eve and Adam had not forgotten their true identity? They wouldn't have gone grasping after that fruit to get something they thought they lacked. They wouldn't then have hidden in shame. They wouldn't then have started blaming each other for what had happened. Not only do they blame each other, but Adam even blames God, saying basically, "This woman you put here with me—she made me do it!" (see Genesis 3:12). He throws both Eve and God under the bus in one fell swoop. What pettiness. What smallness. What fear has overcome Adam to talk like that and genuinely see the world like that? He sounds like a second grader who just got caught breaking something. He sounds like me when I blame others for what has happened and then begin to resent God for setting up the circumstances in which I ended up messing something up of my own volition!

God Doesn't
Cease Reminding Us

In many ways, the rest of the Bible is about the struggle of God's people to remember who they truly are and the problems that ensue when they continue to forget. They act out of jealously, fear, and resentment because they don't remember the truth of their identity. In all kinds of different ways, they try to take matters into their own hands—including literally, when they create idols and start worshipping them instead of the One who created them and loves them personally.

But God doesn't tire of reminding them of the truth. Through Abraham, God lets this little band of peoples know that they belong to him and he belongs to them. And if they stick with him, they will flourish and multiply to become as many as the stars in the sky and the grains of sand on the seashore. And then they forget and end up in slavery. But God seeks them out again. He chooses Moses to lead them to freedom in their homeland but not before going through a trying forty years in the desert. And then they forget once they get to the Promised Land. The commandments were not enough to remind them how to live as God's chosen people. God had to keep sending prophets to remind them who they are and who he is and of the covenant that binds them together in love. But they forget and end up in exile. God reminds them again when he chooses an unlikely candidate, David, to be their king. David flourishes as a just, brave, and faithful king—until he forgets. In his song of repentance for his sin, for separating himself from God by taking advantage of Bathsheba and having her husband killed, he sings, "A clean heart create for me, God; renew within me a steadfast spirit" (Ps 51:10). Make me new. Renew me.

Here is the deep longing of each of our hearts: make me new. In many ways, we tire ourselves out by our selfishness and attempts at self-reliance. It's exhausting and ultimately boring to keep living as the center of the universe. It all gets very small. Somewhere deep down, we want the world to get big again. To be brought back into a place of wonder. Of awe. Of gratitude for our very existence. We want to know that we are loved and cherished. We want to sense that we are special, not when we look in the mirror, but when we are gazed upon from above by God, who created us out of love.

Have there been the moments in your life when things have gotten small and puny because of your self-centeredness or self-reliance? When have you experienced yourself as, in a good way, small and awed by wonder at the world?

Becoming One of Us

So much of the Old Testament follows the same story line: the people of God hear who they are and what their destiny is and then lose track of it again and again, getting themselves into isolation, fear, slavery, exile. Finally, God resorts to something more radical and definitive. He becomes one of them, one of us, so that we can see in the flesh what it looks like to live in freedom and the state of being beloved of God. God becomes man. The Word becomes flesh and dwells among us—first as a baby, then as a child in a forgotten little town, and then, after thirty years, as the savior of humanity.

It is critical to note that before Jesus undertakes his *mission*, his *identity* is first confirmed. Before he begins to proclaim the Gospel, teach, heal, cast out demons, and confront Pharisees, he first allows the Father to confirm him, through the bond of the Holy Spirit, in who he most fundamentally is: beloved Son. His entire mission, therefore, flows from the truth of what is spoken at the Jordan River. The Son is confirmed by the Father as Beloved for all eternity. Of course, Jesus has been hearing who he is for a long time—but it is instructive for us to get a glimpse by way of the scripture of what the Son has been hearing in order for us to know who Jesus really is. From there, it makes more sense how he operates and what the source of his strength, energy, and confidence is.

Jesus is not Superman. He doesn't possess some exotic superpower. The source of his strength is not unique to him. Once he becomes one of us, that same reality becomes a possibility for us. Pope Benedict XVI has indicated that from the moment of baptism, each one of us shares in *the very same relationship* that Jesus has with the Father. When I first read that, I thought it was maybe a typo or a mistranslation. But of course, that's exactly what we believe. That's why God became one of us, so that we can "share in the divinity of Christ who humbled himself to share in our humanity," as the priest says at Mass when he mingles the water with the wine in the chalice on the altar. Jesus possesses only the love of the Father. And the Father is hoping we will receive that love and live out of that love as well.

The whole of Jesus's mission can rightly be seen through the lens of being the beloved Son of the Father. The rest of his work, from his public ministry through his Passion and death, and even the consolation he gives in the Resurrection stories, flows from what is given to him in baptism. The Father calls Jesus his beloved Son, and Jesus then goes out into the world to offer that love to others, that they too might know they are beloved of the Father and in turn offer that love to others. Jesus's mission, given to him by his Father, is to bring the family back together. "Gather to yourself all your children scattered throughout the world," we pray in Eucharistic Prayer III at Mass.

Plunged into the Family of God

Baptism is the sacramental moment, the concrete reality, when incorporation into the family begins. The word "baptize" comes from the Greek word meaning "to plunge." We are, then, plunged into the family of God that is the Church and ultimately into the family that God is in God's very own self: the Father, Son, and Holy Spirit. We are plunged into the Trinity, the set of relationships that constitutes God's very self! So if we get a glimpse into the identity of Jesus in his baptism, when we share in that same baptism, into the life of God, the life of the Trinity, we know from that moment on what our own true identity is and what our mission should look like on a daily basis. Being totally, infinitely loved, and knowing deep down that we are loved, we can move into all of our relationships and activities from that place of knowing, wanting only to bring others into that same knowledge.

I like to remind myself and new parents and families at baptisms, usually of little babies, that the first moment of the Christian life comes with a question from the priest or deacon: "What name do you give this child?" God wants to know, and the whole Church needs to know too. A family member is being added, and we want to know how to call her or him. God wants a real, personal, and particular relationship with this new child of his, and the rest of the brothers and sisters want to know as well. Those moments are so real. So simple. So beautiful. Even if the baby ends up screaming like a banshee through it all, it's real and it's simple. And it's clear as a bell that everyone gathered delights in this baby, and we can only imagine the delight in the heart of God as he gazes from above in those moments.

Then it gets trickier from that moment on, it seems. That clarity gets lost so easily. The pure vision is obscured. Life starts to happen and get in the way. Confusion creeps in. The simple becomes complex. It becomes hard to hear what God says about us and to us.

I have become, you might say, fixated on this vision of the baptism in the Jordan over the years. In my mind, this is almost like the Gospel within the Gospel. The Father tells Jesus who he is. And when we are baptized, from that moment on, the Father tells us who we are as well. You are my beloved daughter. In you I am well pleased. You are my beloved son. In you I am well pleased. It is so simple. I talk about it again and again when I give retreats, do spiritual direction, sit in a confessional. From my perspective, talking to someone, it is plain as day. God sees this person this way. Deep down, this is what God sees and what God proclaims. It is what God is longing for us to believe and what he wants us to receive in our hearts. Not just hear the words, but let the words take over in our hearts and transform everything about us. If we would just *get it*, we would become new! New creations. We would become free. We would have joy. And the difficulties we face in our relationships, our struggles with our own identity, the trouble we make for ourselves because we don't let those words in—all of it would dissipate and get reordered, if we could just *get it*. I wish those I speak with could get it; it's frustrating when they don't. But it's so much easier to see this truth in others. It's awfully difficult to let it into ourselves.

A Fundamental Contemplation

I'm afraid it might take a lifetime to *get it*. But *now* is always a good time to start practicing and try to get back on track. Let me walk you through a brief contemplation of this truth of our lives. It is a vision and a practice worth returning to again and again, one way or another, for the rest of our lives.

Imagine yourself on the bank of the Jordan River. What does the scene look like? Who's there? Is it noisy or quiet? Windy? Sunny and hot? Overcast and cool? Drizzling rain? What does the air feel like on your skin, in your hair? Then look into the river and let your eyes rest on the figure of John the Baptist and whoever else is there. But ultimately, let your gaze focus on the person of Jesus. Behold his face and sense his presence. Once you've "composed the place," as Ignatius describes that use of the imagination in prayer, let Jesus call you into the river. How do you feel when he locks eyes with you and beckons you to come join him?

Allow yourself to wade into the water. You're side by side with Jesus. Maybe you have a brief talk with him. Do you want to say anything to him about how you're feeling? Or maybe you just want to take a moment or two in quiet being in his presence. Soon, though, let Jesus show you how to go down under the water, to descend. Surrender while you descend. While under water, start letting things go. Let go of any uncertainties or anxieties. Let go of fears. Let go of memories of regret, of shame, of inadequacy. Acknowledge places of weakness and let those go. Also, let go of the things you're proud of. Of your accomplishments, your talents, your strengths. The things that you want other people to know about you and think about you, let those go too. Let go of all the good and the bad and the ugly within you. Empty out until you have nothing to show for yourself.

Now let Jesus show you how to rise up out of the water as he stands shoulder to shoulder with you. He too is emptied out. Quiet. Open. Listening. And in that openness, you hear a voice from above, the Father saying to Jesus and through Jesus to you too: "You are my beloved son. You are my beloved daughter. In you, I am well pleased." Let the Father keep saying those words. Try to stay open to hearing them. Let those words penetrate not just your mind, but deeper, into your heart. Let them resonate. Try to stay present and open and receive what the Father says about you and what he says directly *to* you.

Depending on how life has been going lately or even over many years, these words might immediately soak in and be a source of deep consolation, humility, joy, and gratitude. You might want to stay right there and continue to absorb it all and *receive*. That would be ideal! Or you might just let these words in momentarily and get a taste of that consolation. In that case, give thanks even for a fleeting moment of communion and confirmation from God, who looks upon you lovingly and with delight. It might also be the case that these words sound nice, but nothing gets in. That might be frustrating. But it's not the end of the world. The truth of the words remains. This is what God says to us from the moment of our baptism. This isn't just wishful thinking or some made-up self-help exercise. It's what scripture teaches and what the sacraments confer, substantially and definitively. If I can't feel it right now, that's OK. It's still the truth. That's why I really believe this is a go-to contemplation for us, an image for us to remember and return to again and again, probably for the rest of our lives. Our feelings about how those words resonate in us might come and go. The truth remains the same, though. What counts is what God says, how God sees us.

The task is to try to listen, to hear, and to believe what God says to us about who we are. It is essential that we remember. And when we forget, which we will, it is imperative that we place ourselves back in the position of being able to listen, to hear, and to receive. If it's hard to believe at certain times in our lives, that's OK. If we think none of this is true and that surely God either doesn't care or has given up on me, then cast those thoughts out. Those are your thoughts. Those are my thoughts. They are not God's thoughts. God's words are the only ones worth listening to. Way less important, and maybe even deceptive, is what *we think* or how we perceive ourselves. When we start coming up with our own analyses about ourselves, we always get it wrong. It's distorted and will leave us discouraged, sooner or later. When we fall into that trap of monologues with ourselves, in our own heads, I would say we are really letting another voice in, just as Adam and Eve did in the garden. We are letting in a voice that turns us in on ourselves and doesn't lead us out, beyond ourselves, in love. We are letting the evil spirit, the enemy of our true human nature, shape our thinking. Let's turn then in the next chapter to how the voice of the enemy operates both in the Bible and in our own lives. Let's learn the nature of that voice so that we can reject it and come back to the freedom of being beloved of God.

Exercises to Cultivate Habits of Freedom

1. Recall a time in your life when all was well—when things were simple, when you knew you were loved and that you belonged. Look back on that time and savor it. What were the conditions of your life? How was your relationship

with God? Ask God to help you remember and recover the sense you had of yourself at that time.

2. Think about the times you are self-forgetful. What is going on in your life when you are not turned in on yourself—preoccupied, consumed with regret, anxiety, or worry about what other people are thinking, wondering if you are "doing" life right?

3. Recall God's words, "You are my Beloved. In you I am well pleased." What do you need to empty out from inside that will help you hear these words? What are you attached to that prevents you from hearing this clearly?

3

Reject the Lie

"If you are the Son of God . . ."
Matthew 4:3

As you might recall, the scene in the gospels of Jesus's baptism in the Jordan is followed immediately by the temptations in the desert. This is no coincidence. They follow one upon the other. It is one two-part story. And it's not just the story of what Jesus experienced that day two thousand years ago; it's our story as well, today and every day. This two-part story offers us a fundamental paradigm for how to think about the spiritual battle we are constantly involved in, whether we know it or not. The Good Spirit is always aiding us to move in the direction of greater freedom and of faith, hope, and love. And the evil spirit is always moving against us, trying to separate us from others, from ourselves, and from God, the source of that freedom and love. The Holy Spirit is all about union. The evil spirit is all about isolation.

In Ordinary Life

I remember facing a spiritual battle along these lines a few years back. I had been teaching theology at Saint Louis University and was loving it. I was also involved in ministry—giving retreats, doing spiritual direction for a good number of folks, and helping at parishes on the weekends. I thoroughly enjoyed all of it. After a few years of that, though, an administrative job opened up at the university that would involve working across the institution with faculty and staff, helping them learn more about the Catholic and Jesuit aims of the university and also representing the university as a whole, more publicly. I had not thought about doing that job before, but some friends encouraged me to apply. The more I thought about it, I decided that I could actually do a good job there and enjoy the work too. So I applied.

A strange thing happened, however, as the process unfolded. I began to feel anxiety about not getting the job—the same job that had never even occurred to me to apply for only weeks before. I started to get these thoughts of fear and worry about being rejected. That would be not only humiliating for me personally, once I had publicly thrown my hat in the ring, but also disappointing for others who had encouraged me to apply and wanted to see me in that role. I would let them down and be a failure if I didn't get the job. All of a sudden, I had gotten myself strangely tangled up inside and focused inward. What had been a simple opportunity presented for my consideration had quickly become something I was grasping at and clinging to. The freedom I had in entertaining a possibility was becoming a place of a lack of freedom and a focus on myself and how I was perceived. That self-absorption made me feel sick, frankly. It made me feel small, and not in a good way. And I even knew what was going on! I knew the enemy was messing with me—turning a good and exciting, even holy prospect to serve others into an occasion of self-preoccupation. I knew I was being manipulated by the evil spirit, but I could not get myself out of that tangle inside. I don't know that anybody else recognized it. I don't think I was behaving very differently, but interiorly I knew I was *off*.

The experience felt very similar to the days when I was nearing the end of writing my dissertation for a doctorate in theology. Most of the course of my studies was enjoyable. I loved the learning. I didn't have any big plan about what to "do with the degree"; I just knew I wanted to keep studying a while longer. I enjoyed the project I was working on and felt like I was going deeper, just as I wanted. The learning was also helping my prayer and pastoral work and maybe my preaching. It was all good. And then when the conclusion drew near and I faced the prospect of "defending" (what a term!) my work, the anxiety started creeping in. Now the focus wasn't on the work, the ideas, or the learning. Now the focus was on me—how *I* was being judged, how *I* was inadequate, how *I* was probably going to fail, how *I* was maybe going to be rejected. It felt like any moment now I was finally going to be proven to be the fraud I really was. Lots of focus on "I." "Who does he think he is, wanting to have a doctorate and teach in college? He's a fake! There are so many smarter people who are legitimate scholars. What a phony!" Honestly, I felt sick to my stomach when those thoughts and feelings started to come over me.

The self-focus was disgusting and draining. And it undermined the work I was doing fairly well before getting tangled up like that! I started to resent my professors. I resented other students who were smarter than me. I resented the "whole system." I was sucked into feelings of self-pity and blah, blah, blah. And again, I knew in my head the enemy was behind it all. I had a fair amount of experience in talking other people through these kinds of manipulations in my work of spiritual direction, in the confessional, and on retreats. I could read the situation so well for others. From the outside looking in on another, it is often plain as day how the enemy is working and also how the Holy Spirit is gently inviting a person back to simplicity, humility, and confidence. But when it happens to me, even if I *know* in my head what's going on, I have on multiple occasions been helpless to resist it.

Strategies for Battling Through

St. Ignatius gave some good advice for how to deal with moments when we are drawn into an interior battle involving our own thoughts and feelings in addition to the promptings of the Holy Spirit and the undermining attacks of the enemy. In the instances I just described, I knew intellectually that the evil one was toying with me. I knew on some level that I would get through those stretches. But in the moment, it was very tough to get out of that tangle and step back from those mini self-implosions. At the very least in moments like those, it is essential that we not make any significant decisions based on the desolation that we might be experiencing (*Spiritual Exercises* #318).

"Never make a decision in desolation" is a well-known maxim in Ignatian spirituality. It's also pretty good common sense. When we are in desolation, we cannot see clearly. We can't know the truth. We don't have a sense of the whole. We are seeing reality through a particularly narrow lens that is colored by discouragement, fear, and anxiety. We want to get out of the current circumstances. We want to run away, but we don't have a sense of what we want to run *to*. We have lost momentarily a sense of the good we seek, the end for which we have been created, which is love. A total, self-sacrificing love.

So, what to do in the meantime? When I get stuck, when I am in desolation, when I am tangled up inside even if I know in my head I'm being deceived, what to do? If I just try hard to snap out of it, that won't work. If I just think real hard in my own head, trying to figure things out and convince myself of the truth of things, that won't work either. At least not in my experience. I can't *think* my way out of these times. I have to keep acting. I have to keep living. Keep doing the next thing in front of me. Not absolutize things. Not cast judgment on my whole future and get paralyzed by those fears. Not let past hauntings of inadequacy or failure take over my view of the present.

Lessons from Ignatius

Before moving on to look at the temptations Jesus faces in the desert, let's recall briefly a couple more of the rules for discernment of spirits that St. Ignatius offered in the *Spiritual Exercises*. They become especially poignant in this context, I think. As I mentioned in the introduction, it is helpful for our own day-to-day living to keep in mind especially a few of those rules. They remind us what is at work in our interior lives and how those movements shape our exterior lives and behaviors and ways that we see the world.

Ignatius observes, based on his experience of the battle between spirits in his own life, that for the person basically oriented toward union with God and trying to pursue a good life, the enemy instigates "anxiety to sadden and to set up obstacles" to freedom and love. Sometimes a shameful or regrettable moment from our past might flash in our memory, leading to discouragement. We might experience some trigger sparked by what somebody says or does to us. Or perhaps we might experience being dismissed in a way that causes us to go back to a memory where we failed or were left feeling inadequate. That memory can then take over how we think and feel about ourselves in the present. This causes a downward spiral in our interior life, and we feel sadness, shame, and discouragement. Or perhaps some thought about the future overwhelms us and we are led to thinking, "I will never be able to keep up this pathway to God. Who am I kidding? I'm no saint. I'm a failure, a loser, a sinner. God probably doesn't even want me around." The enemy, St. Ignatius explains, "unsettles these persons by false reasons aimed at preventing progress."

For the same person on the path toward God and greater spiritual freedom and love, the Holy Spirit stirs up "courage and strength, consolations, tears, inspirations, and tranquility" (#315). The Holy Spirit often encourages us and gives us strength in a very undramatic and almost unnoticeable way. It is like water being absorbed into a sponge (#335), subtle and discreet. The stronger we are on this pathway, the more we will build up habits of being loving, being focused on the good of others, and of not allowing our egos and self-preoccupations to take over our motivations. As we practice these habits of being, the more solid and stable we become. This way of being becomes natural, as it were, and normal. A characteristic of this way of being is that we are un-self-conscious. We are just living and loving. We are laboring not for ourselves but simply to put the good gifts that have been given to us at work, especially for others. Joy comes with this way of living that is building up relationships, being of assistance to others. This is what it looks like to be authentically human!

Building upon Our Histories

One important key to becoming more attentive to the movements within us is being reflective on a daily basis about what
is happening in the present. Most of our daily life is unfolding
in the midst of different movements of our own thoughts and
feelings, and we typically don't have the time or capacity to
realize what is happening in the moment. For this reason, it is
essential that we form a daily habit of stepping away from the
busyness and (sometimes) inner turmoil of what we are going
through to get perspective on where we are experiencing the
fruitfulness of the movements of the Holy Spirit and where we
are getting tripped up by the evil spirit. Doing a daily examen
gives us the opportunity to pay attention to the multiplicity
of these dynamics so that we can more deliberately focus on
following the encouragement of God and rejecting the manipulations of Satan.

Ignatius describes more fully the texture, as it were, of
these different movements. He urges us to remember the
nature of the consolation we experience when in sync with
the action of the Holy Spirit. It is a "motion in the soul through
which one is moved to love of Creator and Lord." It is fundamentally marked by a posture of humility, knowing that we
are not alone and that we are constantly being invited forward
in reliance on God but also in confidence in God's care and
encouragement. This consolation is sometimes marked by
tears of joy or an overwhelming feeling of goodness, kindness, and beauty that we experience in daily encounters. Most
fundamentally, though, consolation can be detected when
we sense an "increase in faith, hope, and love" as well as an
"attraction to heavenly, eternal goods which produce deep
happiness and peace" (#316). Another way to put it is to look

for the times and circumstances in which our hearts are getting bigger, more selfless, and more confident.

By the same token, it is also important to remember the nature of desolation. When we have allowed ourselves to be tricked or manipulated by the enemy to focus on things other than God and to cast doubt on God's goodness and closeness, we can experience an "obtuseness of soul, turmoil within it," and also an "impulsive motion toward low and earthly things." When we fall into these ruts, we experience in ourselves "feelings that are listless, tepid, and unhappy" (#317). These feelings come because on some level we feel separated from God and, very likely at the same time, separated from ourselves and those around us whom we typically find to be sources of friendship, encouragement, and joy. With these somewhat abstract descriptions in mind, let's move then to the concrete story of Jesus and the temptations he faced from the same enemy and see how we can find ourselves within that story.

Spirits in the River and in the Desert

As we reflected on in the previous chapter, what Jesus experiences in the Jordan River is the confirmation of his primary identity as beloved Son. This is the source of his strength for his mission, and it also shapes the mission itself—to bring all of his brothers and sisters into that same experience of knowing who they are, who we are, beloved daughters and sons of the Father. In all humility and simplicity of heart, Jesus hears and receives those words into the depth of his being. Insofar as Jesus is also the eternal Son of God, he has had much practice in hearing those words and receiving that love from his Father. We are not so practiced. We let a lot of things get in the way of listening and receiving well. Sometimes that is our own doing, but often the enemy uses our experiences, and especially our wounds, against us to distort our ability to hear and to listen to the truth of our identity.

In the story from the gospels, the enemy tries similar tactics against Jesus but fails in the effort. One way to read this story is that Satan pounces immediately on the experience Jesus just had in the river and ever so slightly distorts it in order to drive a wedge between the Son and the Father. He does this in a very subtle way. The first two temptations seem especially tricky to me. Notice that they start with "if." That "if" is part of a strategy to call into question what has already in fact happened. The Father just told Jesus that he is his beloved Son. Period. But the enemy tries to distract from that by introducing a variable, a conditional question that seeks to throw things up for grabs. "*If* you are the Son of God, then turn this stone into bread" (see Matthew 4:3). That is, if you really are who you say you are, then you'd better prove it. Let's see what you've got! There is a kind of taunting involved here. And there is also an effort by Satan to prey upon Jesus's love and devotion, it seems to me.

The temptation is to latch on to the opportunity to defeat the enemy, to prove Satan wrong and show that the Father really does call Jesus his Beloved. Jesus surely would not want the Father to look like a liar. Maybe part of the temptation is to honor his Father by shutting down Satan with a miracle. Maybe there is also a temptation to reveal the power the Father has given him. After all, Jesus is about to start his public ministry where many "signs and wonders" will be shown. Why not start now? There may also be a temptation toward pride cloaked in devotion.

The second temptation is similar. "If you really are the Son of God, then thrown yourself off the parapet of the Temple and see if your Father catches you!" (see Matthew 4:6). Again Satan taunts Jesus and calls into question his relationship with the Father. It is also an even more direct affront to the honor of the Father. *Let's see if he really meant what he said about you. Let's see if he really does love you!* But Jesus does not fall for these manipulations. He doesn't take the bait. He knows who he is and he doesn't need to prove it, and he doesn't need the Father to prove it either. The Father already made the truth abundantly clear in the river. Jesus's belovedness is not in question. He feels no need to prove anything.

In these first two temptations, Jesus allows the enemy to try to drive a wedge between himself and his Father but remains confident in the simple fact of what the Father has already said about his true identity. I think it's interesting how revealing the grammar is here. Let's recall some of those elements of grammar that might sound familiar, especially if you've ever tried to learn another language. In the Jordan River, the Father spoke in the *present tense* and in the *indicative mood*. He stated a fact in the present. There were no conditions set up. He didn't say, *If* you accomplish these things in the future, *then* you will be my Beloved. God speaks eternally in the present tense to us as well. You are, right now, my Beloved. Period. No conditions, no ifs. It is very simple with God.

Conversely, it is characteristic of the enemy to try to make things complex, to lead us into questioning the past (what has already been given) or worrying about the future (whether we succeed at this or that in order to earn or prove God's love for us). We are extremely susceptible to falling for these tricks and manipulations, whereas Jesus was very good at *not* falling for them. He remained simplehearted and confident in what the Father had already told him. He lived in the confidence of the Father's love at every moment—not just at his baptism, but in every moment from then on, all the way to the Cross and beyond.

The third temptation is perhaps the weakest and least subtle of all of them. After being brushed off on the first two, Satan gets desperate. He says, in effect, "If you just worship me, then you can have control over everything and do what you like with all these people" (see Matthew 4:9). Again, though, Jesus resists making this about himself and what he wants to accomplish in his mission. He returns to what is prior— his identity as given by the Father, quoting an ancient word of God from the Old Testament: "The Lord, your God, shall you worship and him alone shall you serve" (Mt 4:10). Pretty straightforward. And thus comes to an end that round of temptations . . . though there will always be more, both for Jesus and for us as well.

Being Deaf to the Call

It is crucial to keep these two scenes, the baptism and the temptations, together when considering our own challenge in discerning spirits. Focusing exclusively on the nature of the temptations we face can get overwhelming and discouraging. It can also be an exercise that is endlessly fascinating. We can get tripped up in so many ways. Things can become so complex and the temptations so nuanced. When we do get fixated on sin or the temptations we face and try to figure out on our own ways to get free of them, even with good intention, we very easily get all tangled up, defeated, and discouraged. That's why it is so important to have the reference point of baptism to go back to. Return to the simplicity of knowing and believing what God has already made clear. But that's easier said than done, I know.

When I try to pray with the scene of the baptism of the Lord, it sounds so good. I really want to hear what the Father has to say to Jesus, and through Jesus, to me. But when I imagine myself going down under the water with Jesus right beside me, when I spend time there, letting everything go, emptying out, and when I come up out of the water and hear those words, ever so subtly I start to talk back. I start to say in my mind and in my heart, unintentionally, something like, "Thanks, Father, for saying that. Thanks for saying I'm your Beloved. But you don't really understand. You don't get it. You must have forgotten about all the bad stuff I've done. All my selfishness. My pettiness, the ways I've hurt other people. The way I constantly put myself and my desires, my interests, first. Thanks for saying I'm your Beloved, but you obviously just don't understand."

In other words, I easily start drifting to the past and dwelling there. Or else I might start focusing on the future. "Thanks for saying that nice thing, Father, about being your beloved son. That sounds great. So, I am going to really start getting my act together, and one of these days, I will really be your beloved son!" And before long, after an initial boost of enthusiasm for getting my act back together, I realize the probability that that won't fully happen. I'll just fall into old patterns of selfishness. Who am I kidding? I'm not going to get any better. I should just accept that I will never really be beloved of God. Or at least I'll never be *worthy* of being beloved. Whether I end up drifting back to regrets and failures from the past or thinking about the insurmountable challenges of the future, I can so easily end up in the same place. Instead of being consoled by this act of prayer, I end up *discouraged*. Exactly the opposite of what I *know* God wants for me, and exactly what I *know* the enemy does indeed want for me! And yet it sometimes goes like that.

Since I've come to realize how I "talk back" in these moments, or rather talk to myself instead of listening to God, two things have become more and more clear to me. One, the Father is speaking to me in the present tense, and yet I shift that encounter in the present to the past or to the future. Sometimes it's too hard to just stay quiet, in the present, and hear what God has to say about me, *right now*, in this moment. I guess it's too vulnerable to stay right there. I don't know. I do know it doesn't come easily. But to deliberately come back again and again to the present is definitely the way forward. God speaks in the present. The enemy usually tries to get us stuck in the past or paralyzed by the future. We allow ourselves to be led into the territory of regrets, shame, the surfacing of old resentments, or discouragement about the possibility of shaking these hindrances in the future. "If only this wouldn't have happened. If only I had not done that. If only that person would not have betrayed me. I should have said this. Or I should have done that," and so on. Lots of "ifs." And none of them deal with the reality at hand, in the present, of being receptive to what God is offering right now.

The other thing that occurs to me when I pray with this scene of the baptism is that my responses, my deflections, sound, at first blush, kind of humble. Maybe even pious. Certainly earnest. "I'm not worthy. You don't understand, Lord, how unworthy I am. I'm no good. I don't deserve that kind of unconditional love from you." Blah, blah, blah. But of course, this isn't humility. It certainly isn't piety. It's telling God, the Creator of the Universe, that he doesn't know what he's talking about. He's wrong and I'm right. I'll determine what's what.

But that's crazy. That's rebelling against God. Who am I to say that God doesn't know what he's talking about? What a dumb thing to say, especially in prayer! But I do that. And I think I'm not alone in this. It's important not to get discouraged if we have the inclination to drift in those directions in prayer. The thing to do, really, is to keep practicing listening to what God says about who we are. Let God define us and give us our true identity. Let our own response come second. Listen and then respond based on what we hear and not what *we* think about who we are. To put it more bluntly, it doesn't matter what I think! And it doesn't matter what you think. It only matters what God thinks. And he calls us his Beloved. Right now. In the present. Our job, first and foremost, is to continue to hear these words, let them soak in, and then begin to live out of the experience of that truth. This is the truth of our identity, and this shapes the nature of our mission in this world.

Practices for
Moving Forward

In the next couple of chapters, I'd like to look at some specific strategies for rejecting the lies of the evil one and returning to the truth. The first way has to do with keeping on talking. It is essential to have good friends or confidants to talk things through with. Only in relationships can we get clarity again. That's the way we're made—to be in relationship with others. To be in relationship with God. So we keep on talking. And also, we keep on living. It is essential to keep acting. Keep taking action in the needs that present themselves to us every day. Over time, both through words and deeds, we can make our way through the sometimes confusing dynamics of the struggles we are in while trying to discern spirits and come to greater freedom and happiness.

Exercises to Cultivate Habits of Freedom

1. Recall an occasion when you were overcome with anxiety or worry about the future. Extend that memory a bit. How did things ultimately turn out?

2. Being completely honest with yourself, consider whether you sometimes pretend to be somebody you're not before God. Do you pretend to be more humble than you really are? More pious?

3. How does God actually see you? Ask him. Get quiet and still and ask with a childlike heart, "Lord, what do you see when you see me? How am I doing?"

4

Talk It Out

"What are you discussing
as you walk along?"
Luke 24:17

A few months into my life as a Jesuit novice, I had a conversation with my spiritual director that I remember very distinctly. We used to meet weekly to talk about my prayer and anything else going on in my life that was affecting my thoughts and feelings. My schedule at that time included daily Mass, weekly spiritual direction, and the careful reading of various documents that govern the way Jesuits operate. And there were lots of conversations with other Jesuit novices. I remember saying to my director something along the lines of, "There sure is a lot of talk about Jesus around here!" Both the Jesuit priests on staff and some other novices spoke freely about their relationship with Jesus.

The thing that made me uneasy, I told my novice director, was actually using the name *Jesus* so often and so freely. I mean I grew up Catholic! Irish Catholic. I was a philosophy major in college and took theology as well. I learned a lot about what the Church teaches about God and so on. But I had kept it all pretty nice and tidy in a set of intellectual categories. I liked to stay in the realm of arguments, ideas, and principles. One of those ideas was about the nature of Christ and how he saves humanity, so I was comfortable with talking about "Christ." That sounded a little more dignified and intellectual. But Jesus? Talking about Jesus made me feel like some kind of televangelist, I told my director. Made me squeamish. He leaned back and howled in laughter. I forget exactly what he said, but the laugh was enough to get the point across. You'd better get used to Jesus! Used to not only talking *about* him but also talking *with* him.

Later that year, when I made the whole of the Spiritual Exercises, I came to know what he meant—though it still isn't easy. I still like the realm of ideas and abstraction. I think that's one reason why the two-part story of the baptism and temptations is so crucial, because it highlights the difference between listening to and speaking with God, through the person of Jesus, and moving out of the dynamic of intimate conversation in order to opt for *thinking* about God and what God may or may not be like and what he may or may not have to say to me directly. It's the same trick the enemy pulled on Eve in the garden. Don't talk to God anymore; just think about him and raise interesting questions and "what ifs."

Living within the Story of God

The story of the baptism and the temptations is so helpful for our own challenges because it is a concrete narrative, with real characters and real movement in the interactions that make up the whole drama of the narrative. The story unfolds in an instructive way. It must be followed through to conclusion.

But this is not just a story to be read, like a novel. It constitutes the "Word of God . . . living and effective, sharper than any two-edged sword" (Heb 4:12).

The story of Jesus's baptism and temptations is intended to capture our minds, hearts, and imagination—to be drawn into, and to be *lived within*, consciously and actively. There's action, but there is also dialogue and communication that drive the story. And we are meant to engage in the same conversation and dialogue from within the story that remains real and true today. In offering strategies for discerning spirits that are based on real practices, I'd like to spend time first on how important speaking and listening are, how important genuine dialogue is, and then turn to the importance of taking action in the following chapter. Words first and then deeds. These two drive our lives forward, and by the same token, the lack of either can stall us and cause us to get closed in on ourselves and paralyzed on the inside.

The Power of a Conversation

Even as I sit down this morning to write, I'm coming off of an excellent conversation with someone. It was the first time we had ever met. We talked about some possible collaborations together in the future. The discovery of common interests, common passions, and a common desire to serve and make a difference in our communities was palpable. I'm on fire at the moment! And it is telling that for several days prior to this, I'd been feeling a bit in a rut. Somewhat stuck. Now, getting into the shortening days of the fall, still in the midst of the COVID pandemic with a possible second wave coming, and personally at a crossroads as to what to give myself to next in my Jesuit life, I have felt like I've been spinning for a while. I miss day-to-day interactions with people, getting energy from others, from conversations, from shared projects and desires. But one conversation just opened up my imagination again and sparked new energy in me. I continue to be amazed at how the right conversation, with the right person, at the right time, can make the world look new again!

As I'm writing while living at Boston College during a sabbatical, I recall also a brief phase some ten years ago when I was here writing my dissertation. I was deep into writing, which is a pretty austere experience. Diving into the readings and the ideas and trying to formulate new insights is, at times, an invigorating, challenging process. But at other times, the isolation of the experience can be too much. It can become overwhelming, even. I remember nearing the end of my writing when I got stuck. I don't remember what the ideas were that I was grappling with, and what I was struggling to formulate in my writing, but I do remember getting stuck. Again, it was palpable. And after a couple of days, I started to panic. I didn't think I was going to break through. I began to doubt the whole project and what it was that I really had to offer in this dissertation. The whole thing started to seem so unimportant and insignificant. Maybe I had been kidding myself the whole time. Maybe this was my Waterloo. I remembered stories of dissertations that never came to completion. ABD. "All But Dissertation" was the dreaded designation that loomed large, and it seemed to be closing in on me!

Out of a sense of desperation and probably more for personal counseling than anything else, I went to visit one of my professors. It had been a while since we sat down and chatted. I had been tucked away in my room with my books and my laptop for some time, and I hadn't been interacting much with others. Not good! I didn't really have any questions for my professor. I didn't have anything in particular to talk about. I just went to see him. Well, it was a very friendly and simple conversation. I honestly don't remember what we even talked about. Maybe a little bit on the project. Maybe some small talk too. But something happened in that brief conversation that snapped me out of it. I rediscovered energy and zeal for what I was working on. The professor showed interest and even delight in some of the work that I was doing, and that woke me up again. I got back on track. Bringing myself and my work back into relationship with another person gave me a whole new sense of energy and creativity.

That is a pretty unimpressive story now that I tell it. Not a lot of color or drama to it. But I do remember that turning point as if it were yesterday. I was beginning to sink into a mini abyss of discouragement and lack of confidence, and all it took to emerge was getting out of myself and engaging in a conversation with a trusted friend and mentor. That was enough. I don't think he had any especially good insights for me; it was the act of the conversation itself that opened me up again and made possible a new beginning. Ironically, the whole point of my dissertation was to demonstrate the centrality of *dialogue* to Joseph Ratzinger's (the future Pope Benedict XVI) way of doing theology. In fact, the whole of Christian theology is dialogical. Speaking and listening. Engaging with the Other. Becoming who we truly are in the midst of dialogue. That was the argument around which my dissertation revolved, and yet I failed to keep living it in the midst of the thinking and writing! Lesson learned. For the time being.

On the Road,
Speaking and Listening

Another important gospel passage drives this point home and provides a useful paradigm for how to imagine our daily lives when it comes to this need for dialogue. Just as the baptism and the temptations of Christ are gospel frameworks for how to consider our true identity and mission and how that identity and mission can be hindered by the temptations of the enemy, the story of Emmaus gives us a way of considering how we can maintain our center of gravity from day to day.

Near the end of his gospel, Luke offers us this story of one of the occasions of Jesus's interaction with others after his suffering, death, and Resurrection. Curiously, it is the longest, most detailed account of all the Resurrection appearances Jesus made. All of these Resurrection accounts reveal how Jesus continues to fulfill the mission given to him by his Father. Now, the task is to bring consolation and hope to those of his friends who are trapped in fear, isolation, and discouragement. He wants to draw them back into the confidence that comes with being his friend.

Having just described Mary Magdalene telling the other disciples about the empty tomb she discovered and Peter and John witnessing the same thing, the gospel account takes a major twist. The empty tomb calls into question, in a good way, the narrative that the disciples had come to believe. That Jesus is dead and it's all over. That their previous hopes had fallen apart. But now the tomb is empty, so maybe there's a different story unfolding. The radical destabilization that began for the disciples in witnessing the death of Jesus now brings another moment of uncertainty. And then Luke turns to a different story: "Now that very day two of them were going

to a village seven miles from Jerusalem called Emmaus, and
they were conversing about all the things that had occurred"
(Lk 24:13–14). On that same day, these disciples were walking
away from Jerusalem, where it had all happened, and they are
going back to where they had come from. Deflated. But along
the way, they are interrupted. More destabilization!

"And it happened that while they were conversing and
debating, Jesus himself drew near and walked with them, but
their eyes were prevented from recognizing him. He asked
them, 'What are you discussing as you walk along?' They
stopped, looking downcast" (24:15–17). Maybe I'm projecting
here, but when I read that the disciples are "conversing and
debating," I imagine them muttering. It's the kind of conversation that is not lifting them up but instead taking them down.
When Jesus interrupts them, they stop, "looking downcast."
It seems that the conversation and debates they were engaged
in did not reveal greater perspective and provide encouragement but were more like an echo chamber that leads to wallowing. Maybe they were gossiping and lashing out at others
who did this to their friend. Maybe they were feeling sorry for
themselves. Maybe they were playing out worst-case scenarios
about what might now happen to them since they knew the
one who had been publicly executed. Their conversation could
have been any combination of these things. But the point is,
it was not a conversation that was leading them forward in
encouragement, but rather the opposite. It was the kind of
talking that was causing them to turn in on themselves. The
kind of conversation that the enemy loves to see us get drawn
into. The kind of conversation that leads to isolation.

And then Jesus poses a simple question: What are you
talking about among yourselves? I think this is a great take-
away question for all of us in our daily lives. Let Jesus ask

us that question every day. "So, what are you talking about?" Especially when we are muttering to ourselves and being drawn into discouragement, resentment, fear, or anxiety. Let Jesus interrupt that monologue and draw you out of yourself and into a dialogue, a two-way conversation. That's key. Because once we start talking to him and not to ourselves, the fog that surrounds us lifts and we begin to see clearly.

When the disciples respond, you can hear the bitterness or pain or maybe anger in their voices: "One of them, named Cleopas, said to him in reply, 'Are you the only visitor to Jerusalem who does not know of the things that have taken place there in these days?'" (Lk 24:18). If I used that tone with just about anybody, that person would understandably edge away. Who wants to talk to someone crabby like that? But Jesus hangs in there with them. He takes that bitterness from them, responding with patience and gently probing a bit deeper:

> And he replied to them, "What sort of things?" They said to him, "The things that happened to Jesus the Nazarene, who was a prophet mighty in deed and word before God and all the people, how our chief priests and rulers both handed him over to a sentence of death and crucified him. But we were hoping that he would be the one to redeem Israel; and besides all this, it is now the third day since this took place. Some women from our group, however, have astounded us: they were at the tomb early in the morning and did not find his body; they came back and reported that they had indeed seen a vision of angels who announced that he was alive. Then some of those with us went to the tomb and found things just as the women had described, but him they did not see." (Lk 24:19–24)

And so the dialogue really begins. They start to tell Jesus how they see the world right now. They acknowledge the hopes they previously had in Jesus and the confidence that they were really going somewhere, that God was doing something through Jesus and Jesus had been including them in it! But then it all fell apart. Maybe it would have been better if they had never been invited into that friendship in the first place. This was a wound in their own lives that might well not ever be healed.

Even though the disciples say the women in their group had "astounded" them, they don't seem too astounded to me, because they are proceeding as though all is lost. Even if the women were trying to tell them otherwise, they obviously are not at a point of really believing them . . . yet. They are still stuck in their grief and loss and maybe self-pity. But at least now they are talking in a way that has the potential to move them forward. They have laid out on the table what they are really thinking and feeling in that moment. And they are talking to some One who can lead them, as opposed to talking to themselves, which leads to smallness of heart and discouragement.

Once they've gotten these things off their chests and have told Jesus how they see the world at the moment, now they are also ready to hear a different word in response. After offering their perspective, the disciples seem to experience a moment of vulnerability in which they are open to having that perspective altered, broadened, brought into better focus. The opening is there for Jesus to shed light, to fill out the picture, to help them see the bigger reality and begin to grasp what God has actually been doing in the midst of all the violence and loss and pain.

> And he said to them, "Oh, how foolish you are!
> How slow of heart to believe all that the proph-
> ets spoke! Was it not necessary that the Messiah
> should suffer these things and enter into his glory?"
> Then beginning with Moses and all the prophets,
> he interpreted to them what referred to him in all
> the scriptures. As they approached the village to
> which they were going, he gave the impression
> that he was going on farther. But they urged him,
> "Stay with us, for it is nearly evening and the day is
> almost over." So he went in to stay with them. And
> it happened that, while he was with them at table,
> he took bread, said the blessing, broke it, and gave
> it to them. With that their eyes were opened and
> they recognized him, but he vanished from their
> sight. (Lk 24:25–31)

The back-and-forth of their conversation, together with the walking, the invitation to stay for dinner, and the ultimate moment of the breaking of the bread, converge to set the conditions for something new to happen to the disciples. Despite the apparent certainty of their worldview, an opening emerges, thanks in large part to the vulnerability they feel after their conversation with Jesus. The conditions are right for them to be open to the possibility of a new vision, a new understanding, a new horizon.

The disciples' eyes are opened because of the dialogue they had been engaged in—not unlike Mary Magdalene, in a different Resurrection narrative, who could *see* Jesus only once she *heard* her name spoken by him. I don't know exactly what to make of these instances of seeing more clearly as a result of speaking and listening. One sense opens up the other. But it is fascinating.

And maybe it resonates for you. Having talked out, with God or a good friend or family member, something that had been nagging at you and dragging you down, haven't you felt as if the world literally looked different afterward?

With Dialogue
Comes Freedom

More than once I've had the experience, in the confessional or a spiritual direction situation, where a person with a great burden says something out loud, usually something quite judgmental about themselves or someone else, and then immediately starts laughing. The burden just seems to melt away once they get that crazy thought that has been plaguing them in their heads out into the open. And when those distorted thoughts are spoken out loud and the laugh comes, so does the beginning of a broader, clearer, more accurate view of the world. And peace comes too. Not that all the problems are fixed, but peace comes as we realize that our problems are not as overwhelming as we once thought and that we are not alone in facing them, whatever they might be. Our relationship with the person we are having the conversation with, as well as our relationship with the God who loves us and is on our side, becomes a source of calm and confidence for what lies ahead once the conversation concludes and the time for action emerges.

Tell Me What Happened

A very ordinary and mundane human experience illustrates the effectiveness of this need to speak out how we see things. Parents, and maybe moms especially, get plenty of practice in this territory with their kids, especially little kids. And they handle these situations seemingly instinctually. In those very common occurrences when a child gets hurt—trips and falls, falls off a bike or out of a tree, skins a knee or hands—it is kind of neat to see and hear how many moms respond on the spot. I've experienced it myself and seen many moms do it.

When the crying kid comes into contact with Mom, Mom brings the child into her arms, probably gives them a kiss on the head, and then says something like it's OK, you're OK. A question soon follows: "Tell me what happened. Tell Mama what happened." On the one hand, that seems like a pretty silly thing to ask. Of course, Mom knows what happened. Mom usually knows everything that has happened! I don't think they teach this at mom school, but as an outsider to this dynamic, I find it interesting to note what flows so naturally out of the mom's mouth: "Tell me what happened." She knows the child needs to explain it, to speak it out, to give their own perspective. Somehow, through the tears and the crying, sometimes with gasping between breaths, a child never hesitates to give voice to their experience. How good it is that Mom is asking me what happened! She cares. She wants to know. And I can tell the one who loves me most how much pain I am in, how hard my life is at the moment! The child may even play it up a bit to give more drama to the situation. But the most important thing is that there is a chance now to speak out how they feel and what their situation is. And in that speaking out, the healing is already beginning to happen. The gasping for air is subsiding, the flow of tears is abating, the volume of the voice is softening. Things are already getting better, between being held and loved and having someone to speak with and to be heard by and to experience that pure love and concern in response.

Maybe it's a bit like that with God. To me, that story of the disciples on the way to Emmaus reveals a God, in the flesh in the person of Jesus, who does the very same thing. He appears when we are hurting and afraid and confused and asks us to "tell me what happened." What are you talking about as you go along the way? Tell me how you see things and how you feel about them and what your thoughts are right now, in this moment. Even though Jesus knows—after all, God knows what we're going through at every moment—it is still important for us to tell him, to give voice to it all. Only when we do that do we begin to be opened up to hear a different word in response. When he speaks back, he takes seriously where we are right now but also fills in the rest of the story. He reminds us of the whole. In the moment of pain and frustration, our views can get very narrow, focusing only on what has gone wrong. That darkness can become totalizing for us. But once we have spoken, we are ready, perhaps, to be given once again a sense of the whole. Our pain or frustration doesn't go away, but it is situated in a much larger context now. And we are made ready to see more clearly from that point on, to take some next steps forward instead of going backward to feel sorry for ourselves and wallow in our defeats. We are ready to move out of our temporary paralysis and forward to live in freedom, to get out of ourselves and start living with others, living and loving.

Going Out of Ourselves

To return briefly to the story about the disciples on the way to Emmaus, it is worth remembering how that story ended with a new beginning. The disciples didn't just have their vision cleared up. Once they recognized Jesus in the breaking of the bread and he then vanished from their sight, what's the very next thing that happens? They make a U-turn and go back to Jerusalem to tell the others what they had seen. They become apostles—sent by the risen Jesus to go and tell the Good News and encourage others in their same state of being afraid, paralyzed, and perhaps wallowing in resentment or self-pity. "Then they said to each other, 'Were not our hearts burning [within us] while he spoke to us on the way and opened the scriptures to us?' So they set out at once and returned to Jerusalem where they found gathered together the eleven and those with them who were saying, 'The Lord has truly been raised and has appeared to Simon!' Then the two recounted what had taken place on the way and how he was made known to them in the breaking of the bread"(Lk 24:32–35).

This is almost the end of the Gospel of Luke. The next scene, which concludes the gospel, has Jesus promising to the apostles the coming of the Holy Spirit. The author of the Gospel of Luke is the same as that of the Acts of the Apostles. So the conclusion of the gospel of Jesus in Luke moves directly into the gospel of the Holy Spirit, as Acts of the Apostles is sometimes called. There, the story of the unfolding of the life of the early Church through the proclamation and ministry of the apostles and earliest followers of Jesus takes shape. It is the story of the phenomenal growth of the Church, sparked by the witnesses to the risen Jesus now empowered by the Holy Spirit and living in the true freedom of the children of God. This, too, is our story. We who are witnesses to Jesus are empowered by the same Holy Spirit two thousand years later. And the movement of that Spirit upon us is always to move us beyond ourselves, into the world, to share in the mission of Jesus to make his love known, to encourage those who need it, and to serve those in need. The discernment of spirits, then, always ultimately leads us not into further introspection, but outward into action and into love. It's to that "final" phase of discernment that we turn now.

Exercises to Cultivate
Habits of Freedom

1. Think about the times you are most ornery or crabby during the day. What are you saying to yourself in those moments? What is the lie you are subtly allowing the evil one to get you to believe about yourself?
2. Take time to do some deeper remembering and reflecting on the early experiences of your life. Were there any hurts, disappointments, failures, or betrayals that have led to you believing this lie?
3. Say that lie about yourself out loud to Jesus or to a good friend. Does it sound silly? Good! Let it sound silly, again and again.

5

Go on Offense

"Do you love me? . . .
Feed my sheep."
John 21:17

So far in this book we have focused on coming to a fuller vision by way of habits of reflection and the recognition of how discernment of spirits can provide ways forward for us, to greater freedom. These habits of reflection, of remembering who we truly are, of practicing dialogue with God and those around us, are essential. And it's also the case that life goes on regardless of how we are interpreting the experiences of every day and how attentive we are to the movements of the Holy Spirit and the manipulations of the evil one. Life goes on, and we have work to do. There are tasks before us. Choices to make. Life to live. I'd like to turn now from the focus on introspection and interiority of the previous chapters to a vision that is outward oriented and opened up to experience and life in a renewed way. It is, after all, in that outward focus and living of life's experiences on a day-to-day basis that we can seek and hopefully *find* God in all things. And as we do so, we can begin all over again the process we've been exploring: being opened up in unsettling circumstances, being reminded of who we truly are, rejecting lies about ourselves, and talking out the circumstances of our lives with God and others in order to get perspective on what we experience in ordinary life.

Taking the Risk to Go Outside of Ourselves

My cousin Camille was quite a character. She was totally alive and very much free. One of my favorite stories of hers was one she shared when she became a new mom. She had brought home her new baby, Lainey, whom she had been hoping and praying for for years. She finally had been given the great gift of her life, and she had her precious infant all to herself, at home. For the time being, she took leave from teaching, about which she was also passionate. She was passionate about a lot! So life was looking great. But after a few months, Camille started to feel a little cooped up in the suburbs of Minneapolis and St. Paul. She loved every moment of the day with Lainey, but she was also starting to miss interaction with other people. Her husband was of course supportive, but he worked all day. She planned outings and activities with Lainey, but she was getting lonely and just needed a friend. So she went and found one.

As she described it later on, Camille spotted another gal around her age in the neighborhood that she had recently moved to. This neighbor also had a baby. Sometimes they would cross paths out on the street pushing their strollers and smile and say hi. This other young woman seemed good to Camille. Normal. Maybe fun. And she seemed like another mom who might also be feeling cooped up lately. So, after doing some reconnaissance for a couple weeks and spotting where the other gal lived, Camille walked up to her front door one day and rang the doorbell. As her neighbor answered the door, Camille stuck out her hand and said, "Hi, I'm Camille. I'm going to be your new best friend!" And as only Camille could work this kind of magic, they did indeed become great friends.

It sure helps me to remember that story. It's a great icon for me. Plenty of times along the way at different times in my life, I have been drawn into inertia, social and otherwise. When I was a pastor on the Pine Ridge Indian Reservation, the mission where we lived and where the internet worked and where there was food in the fridge was twenty or thirty miles from the various parishes I was responsible for. Early on, I tried to be professional and organized and decided to write articles for the Sunday bulletin, which about thirty people might receive at church. God knows if anybody actually read them. I told myself that certain days would be better spent staying at the mission and doing email, writing copy for the bulletin, and keeping up with paperwork, not that there was much of it to do.

Those days when I stayed at the mission to work always left me feeling pretty crummy by the time the evening came around. I would be lethargic and not enthusiastic about much. After several months of those experiences, when I was inclined to stay at the mission and "do work," I forced myself instead to get in the car and drive around. I could always come up with someone to visit. I could go to Big Bats and buy a pack of cigarettes. I could go to Pinky's store and buy a donut and coffee and see who was hanging around in the parking lot. I could also swing through the hospital waiting room; there was always a good chance I'd know someone there and could break up their wait time a bit. Every once in a while, I would stumble onto a family situation where I discovered something important that I wouldn't have known about otherwise. Those days when I just headed out and cruised around to see who I would run into turned out to be the best. When it would have made more "sense" to stay home and sit in the office, I instead went out and found countless graces off the compound, out there, beyond myself. Getting out there every day and interacting with friends and meeting new people and discovering new needs among the people reminded me what I was there for in the first place. And it gave me energy for the next day and very concrete things to follow up on with folks.

I gained a similar insight one day earlier on as a Jesuit novice when I was teaching at our school on the Pine Ridge. The teaching had not been going well for a whole host of reasons. Maybe first, I wasn't a very good teacher! But there were lots of other layers of obstacles as well. The Pine Ridge is home to the Oglala Lakota people. They were a fierce warrior people when they started interacting with the white settlers and ultimately the US Army in the nineteenth century. Soon after those first exchanges, the government began to take their land away because of the discovery of gold in the Black Hills. Many battles and significant violence ensued, including the massacre at Wounded Knee in 1890, the last major battle between the US Army and a Native American tribe. A lot of trauma persists on the reservation, rooted in this painful history and exacerbated further by the serious substance abuse problems that affect, one way or another, every family living there today. In that context, I was hoping that I could be a good teacher for the kids and especially give a sense of the care of God and the light of Christ's tenderness in their lives as they face so many challenges. And yet, the teaching, as I say, was not going well. I wasn't getting through effectively.

When Ash Wednesday came around, we planned to have a small, intimate Mass for each class to begin the season of Lent. I was hopeful that these might be prayerful and renewing moments for the students, but also, frankly, for myself. I was getting a little burned out, and I sure wanted some spark, some light in my own life and heart at that time. So we went ahead with the Masses held in a makeshift chapel, which was really just a drab conference room. It was dreadful. Each Mass was more frustrating than the last one, and they went on throughout the day. The kids were disrespectful and self-conscious and acted like pretty typical teenagers being forced to attend Mass for reasons not totally clear to them. In hindsight, I can see how this whole approach was not well conceived. For one thing, we hardly ever had school Masses there, and the students had not been well introduced or habituated into the benefit of these times of prayer together and the reception of the sacraments. But I didn't appreciate the lack of preparedness of the students, which was not their fault. I just wanted this to "work." And it didn't. And I got angry. I was extremely frustrated as the day wore on.

Finally, 3:00 came and it was mercifully over. When it was all done, I was so mad that I just had to get off the compound of that school. I beelined for the car and headed into town to Big Bats to buy a pack of cigarettes. My plan was to mope and brood for the rest of the afternoon, feeling sorry for myself and muttering about my woes.

But my moping was interrupted. While I stood in line, I was approached by Delayne. He was a young man who was omnipresent in the town of Pine Ridge. He was born with fetal alcohol syndrome, meaning he was essentially poisoned in the womb because of his mother's alcoholism. As a result, he was stunted a bit in his physical growth and significantly so in his

mental and intellectual development. He could not communicate well, but he loved being around people and approached
everyone eagerly, often giving extremely forceful hugs, which
also got him into trouble. In fact, as I came to know, he was
often severely mistreated and beaten up around town because
he was so vulnerable and unprotected. But he kept on getting
out there and interacting with everyone he came across.

Well, Delayne came up to me that day, after the series of
disasters at school. And just when I was ready to dig into an
excellent moping and self-pitying session on my own, Delayne
broke through that and interrupted my plan. He came alongside me in the line and proceeded to give me a very strong hug
around my waist as he looked up at me and said, "You're my
friend!" I tried to get out of his hold, but he held on tighter.
When I got back into the car, I just had to laugh. The Holy
Spirit, in the form of Delayne, had broken through into my
heart at just the right time, when I was ready to shut down. It
was a very strange and effective gift to receive that day. And
a great way to begin Lent. I had just heard proclaimed five or
six times at the Masses earlier in the day the first line from the
first reading from the prophet Joel. "Even now," said the Lord
to me multiple times through those readings, "return to me
with your whole heart" (Jl 2:12). Now is not the time to close
in on yourself. Now is the time to open up. And so, for a time,
I opened up, not because I made the choice to do so interiorly, but because Delayne broke in on me from the outside.
Because he went out of himself that day, I was forced out of
myself as well. As I let that little moment soak in while sitting
in the car afterward, I laughed and maybe also cried a little.
But one thing is for sure—my heart was lighter and freer, and
I was, for a little while, surprised by the joy that comes from
not turning in on myself.

Contemplation in Action

These little life experiences speak to another well-known slo-
gan of Ignatian spirituality. Ignatius admonishes the Jesuits
that they must become "contemplatives in action." It is pre-
sumed that Jesuits will be actively engaged in the world and
not just in spiritual or "churchy" activities. Our work leads
us to teach chemistry, advocate for the poor, create art, run
complex, multimillion-dollar educational institutions, and
discover new materials in space, among other things. In the
midst of that activity, much of which is secular in nature, the
challenge and opportunity is always to step back every day
and contemplate the reality and the action of God's presence
in the midst of all things. All things can be seen in the light
of the sacredness of God's providence and creation. "Nothing
human is foreign to us, because nothing is merely human," as
the playwright Terence said and which inspired Jesuits early
on in their labors. This is an ongoing "iterative" process as
people like to say today. The more action we engage in, the
more there is to contemplate and come to a sense of wonder
about; and the more wonder, joy, and gratitude we experience
in that contemplation, the more energy we have to reengage
in the world and labor on its behalf.

The Canadian Jesuit philosopher of the twentieth century,
Bernard Lonergan, neatly described the structure of human
consciousness that speaks to this way of being and learning
and living. It is not limited to Jesuits. It is most profoundly
human! Roughly, the structure is as follows. First, we always
start with *experience*. We don't have clear, distinct ideas in
our heads that tell us how to live and how to go about our
daily activities. We start with the stuff of basic, concrete experiences. We see, we look, we hear, we smell, we touch, and
so on. Life and reality come to us through our senses. From

those experiences, we necessarily move into the inclination to *understand* what just happened, especially if the experience captivated or jarred us on some level. I hear a boom outside my window that was singular and unexpected. The noise gets picked up through my hearing, but then I naturally want to look outside and see what happened. I want more experience to confirm the first experience. And then I want to piece together things to understand what happened. Was it thunder? A car crash? Did someone just launch a potato gun? It would be nice to know. It would be interesting to know. I want to know! Based on my understanding that starts to take shape, I then move into a different stage. I might be in a situation where a *judgment* is called for. If it was thunder, I might need to make some plans for the near future. I might delay going out or decide to bring an umbrella. If it was a car crash, I might want to run out and see if anyone was hurt and if I can help. If it was a potato gun, I might need to get out there and see if I can launch one too before they go back inside! Flowing from that judgment that comes from my understanding of the experience, the final move is to *act*. Based on the nature of the judgment, I may or may not be moved into action. And once I move into whatever action that might be, the whole process starts over again. I have new experiences in light of my decision to act in one way or another and then try to understand those experiences, adjust judgments about how to proceed, and so on.

This is the dynamic we are living without being too conscious of it. We are constantly taking in new experiences and shaping perspectives and judgments about the world and how we fit into it. It's pretty easy to get into certain ruts in this regard and not allow our vision to broaden or be refined. Being deliberate and intentional about the reflective dimension of these processes is our opportunity to come alive more fully and live lives worth living. Lives that are energizing and life-giving and interesting. The ruts can occur, though, especially when we gradually begin to close ourselves off from new experiences. Whether by inertia or memory of past experiences or fear of what might happen in uncertain circumstances, we can so easily begin to narrow our horizons and possibilities, and our worlds can get pretty small. And then interiorly, we can become bored or resentful about our circumstances or any number of other responses that come when life seems bland and repetitive. We do well then, especially when life starts to get kind of flat, to make that extra push to go outside of ourselves, to take some risks in encountering the world and other people, and then see what happens.

In Lockdown

As I write this, I am conscious of what a unique time this has been in the midst of the COVID-19 lockdowns we have been experiencing as a country and even as a global community. It truly has been a challenge to remain concretely engaged with other people and with real, authentic human activity and to be outward focused when so much has demanded that we remain locked away and distant from one another. I can't wait until this is over. As is true for everyone, I so much look forward to becoming free again and able to get out and about and have those everyday human encounters again. Zoom meetings are fine, but they are no substitute for face-to-face human interaction. I hope we still know how to do it. How to live. How to get beyond ourselves, to reach out, to love and to be loved in the concrete circumstances of daily life. Hopefully, we will be moved to double down on these outward movements beyond ourselves and come to a whole new experience of what it is to

live and to love. And if we have become accustomed to staying away from others out of fear or if we have become stuck
or depressed as a result of these many months of isolation, I
pray that the Holy Spirit comes in power to bring us out of
ourselves and into communion with one another like never
before.

Agere Contra

These pretty ordinary examples of inertia on the one hand,
and sources of energy on the other, bring to mind one of the
important takeaways from the *Spiritual Exercises*. One of
those rules for discernment of spirits that St. Ignatius offers
is the admonition to, at times, "go against." The Latin phrase
is *agere contra*. Specifically, this is a strategy to keep in mind
when we are stuck in desolation. In those circumstances, the
enemy coaxes us to stay right where we are, lethargic, maybe
depressed, anxious, and worried to such a degree that we get
paralyzed by turning in on ourselves. In those times, the Holy
Spirit wants to snap us out of it and get us out of ourselves, and
we can cooperate with that plan. Ignatius encourages us that
in those moments it is "profitable to make vigorous changes in ourselves against the desolation" (#319). It might mean
doing some fasting or abstaining from something we have
grown comfortable with, like skipping dessert or a meal, or
consciously spending more time in prayer than we normally
would even though prayer has become dry.

"Going against" can also take the form of concrete, out-
ward-facing actions. It might mean extra efforts at generosity
or kindness. Or, as my mom used to say, "Quit moping around
the house, feeling sorry for yourself, and go do something for
somebody!" Or as her dad used to say to her and her seven
siblings, "Go outside, run around the block, and blow the stink

off you!" That's one down-home way to think about conduct-
ing spiritual warfare on a daily basis. The enemy can ever so
subtly get a bit of a stranglehold on our desires and ways of
seeing the world. We can be manipulated into discouragement. And sometimes it takes going on offense to shake off
the enemy, so that we can get back on track with living and
loving as we are made to do.

Called Out of Ourselves

When it comes to our spiritual lives, and especially as our
lives get played out in very mundane ways, we are confronted
almost nonstop with decision points about how we are going
to respond and act or not act, depending on the situation.
As we have noted earlier, life happens, we have experiences
and encounters with others every day, and sometimes those
experiences throw us for a loop. They hit a nerve that reminds
us perhaps of an old wound or an old lie that we had become
accustomed to believing about ourselves. And believing those
lies, over time, leads to a propensity to fall into ourselves. In
fact, according to St. Augustine, that's what the nature of sin is.
He called it the inclination to become *incurvatus in se*—caved
in on ourselves.

In light of those challenges, the Lord continues to seek us
out and call us out of those caves, as it were. But the Lord also
takes seriously our need to continue to be healed interiorly
so that we can become truly free. He is not training us to be
stoics, to just toughen up and move on with life. There's a little
bit of that, but it runs deeper.

Another one of the Resurrection narratives from the Gospel illuminates this dynamic between the Lord and us most
poignantly. After his Passion and death, after having been
abandoned by his friends who had scattered in fear, Jesus,

breaking out of the tomb and rising from the dead, has more to do. He continues that mission given to him by his Father, and strengthened by the movement of the Holy Spirit, to console and to empower his friends. And it is the same Holy Spirit that empowers us and encourages us to do the same Father's will in our lives. In his resurrected state, Jesus carries on his mission of bringing back together those who have been scattered, starting with those who had been closest to him. We already talked about Mary Magdalene and the disciples on the way to Emmaus. Let's consider now the story of Jesus and Peter on the seashore.

Do You Love Me?
Feed My Sheep

Remember the scene. Peter and the others had gone back to fishing in the wake of the death of their friend. Even though they had reason to believe he might be alive after all, they were back out on the sea, fishing. They still had to live and make a living. And as they came in that morning to the shore, Jesus was waiting for them and cooking for them. It's a very concrete, simple scene as conveyed in scripture, probably resembling many meals that Jesus had shared during his ministry along the shore. And in that familiar setting, Jesus pulls Peter aside. He needs to have a brief but tough conversation with him. Not to reprimand him, but to bring him back to life.

The three times Jesus asks Peter, "Do you love me?" (Jn 21:15–17) obviously echo the three times Peter had denied Jesus only a few days earlier during his arrest and suffering before the Crucifixion. No doubt Peter carried an immense amount of shame because of his failure to stand up to the maidservant, despite his understandable fear of the crowds that were watching and listening to see if he was associated with Jesus, who was viewed as a criminal and a threat to the local power of the scribes and Pharisees and also the Roman officials. Who knows how conscious Peter was of that interior shame in that moment on the shore when Jesus starts asking him questions? But as Jesus persists, it is clear that he is hitting a nerve. Peter, "distressed" at being asked a third time, responds, perhaps with some fear, anxiety, and agitation. "Of course I love you!" Perhaps he was getting indignant, even. It's a bit painful to watch and to listen to this scene, knowing the raw state Peter is in in his recently failed discipleship. It even seems perhaps a little cruel on the part of Jesus to probe like this. But he is, of course, not doing this to rub Peter's nose in his failures. He is doing this because he knows the shame in Peter that needs to come up to the surface and be healed. And the only way to confront that need is for Peter to go through the discomfort of facing those failures in all his vulnerability. Once that shame comes up to the surface and is confronted, though, Jesus does effect exactly that healing.

It is important to note just how Jesus offers that healing. It's a twofold process. He doesn't say, "Don't worry about it, Peter. That's all water under the bridge. Let's just move on." He doesn't discount what happened. Besides, that would not bring about real healing anyway. Peter might just be ladened with more guilt if Jesus were that cavalier about it. He would feel an even greater distance from Jesus if Jesus nonchalantly waved a hand and dismissed his egregious failure. The healing needs to go deeper. Jesus exposes Peter where he needs to be exposed, in the context of asking whether or not he loves him. His question also situates the whole of their relationship in the context of that love rather than failure or success at being courageous and loyal.

Once Peter has a chance to respond yes, Jesus immediately takes his word for it and calls Peter out of himself and his shame. He gives him a job: "Feed my sheep" (Jn 21:17). The prior words needed to be spoken and heard, but the nature of their relationship moves in that moment from an exchange in words into the realm of deeds, of shared labor and mission. Jesus sends Peter, and by extension us, out on a mission. He urges us to get out there and feed his sheep every day. He's begging us not to get turned in on ourselves. He knows it will do us no good, and in the meantime, others need help. They need someone to break in on their lives too, so that they can come out of themselves. And as we are sent out into the world, so begins anew our pathway. We begin again to experience life, maybe to encounter great beauty and joy, and maybe to be thrown for a loop again, but no matter what we experience, the Lord will be present, walking alongside us, asking if we love him and whether we will help feed his sheep by our lives.

Exercises to Cultivate
Habits of Freedom

1. Recall the particular circumstances of your life when you've allowed yourself to get stuck in desolation. What signs did you miss or not pay attention to that indicated you were about to get stuck?
2. Think of how you have gotten out of desolation in the past. What has been a good strategy for you that is similar to St. Ignatius's encouragement to "go against" (*agere contra*)?
3. Reflect on the last week or so. Call to mind an experience when you were "interrupted" by somebody or some activity you weren't expecting. Was there a grace moving

in the midst of that? Was God somehow communicating his presence to you in the midst of that interruption?

Conclusion

Living Lives of Love, Freedom, and Joy

After the Crucifixion, the disciples were in a very fragile spot. We spoke at the beginning of this book about the reality of becoming decentered. For the disciples, this was perhaps *the* defining moment of being decentered in the course of their lives. And yet, they had experienced uncertain circumstances since the moment they had met Jesus. From the day Jesus called each of them by name, he had led them out of places of comfort and stability. That call continued as he led them into situations of preaching the Good News to those who had been shut out, feeding the hungry, praying over people who needed to have evil spirits cast out, and healing those who were desperately ill. And he brought them along with him into unsettling and even scary situations when he was confronting the chief priests, scribes, Pharisees, and other people who were using their power corruptly. The disciples were very familiar with being destabilized in the midst of their following of Jesus.

But that immediate stretch after the Crucifixion and death of their friend and Lord was a moment of destabilization like no other. In the immediate aftermath they were obviously afraid, and they found each other and gathered, just to be together. And Jesus came into their midst repeatedly bidding them peace (see John 20:19, 21). That was the essence of his

81

ministry in the wake of his death and Resurrection—to go to his disciples, to meet them in their fear and isolation, and to give them courage, to en-courage them. He personally seeks them out in instances when they don't even know what to seek or what to ask for. And yet in the midst of these experiences, more and more, they find their true center, their place of genuine stability, in the confidence that comes with friendship with the same Jesus.

Waiting to Be Found

A well-known Jesuit retreat director once told a story that left a wonderful and unsettling vision in my own imagination. He is blind and is also incredibly competent at making his way around in all kinds of different settings. In fact, when I was a first-year Jesuit novice, he came through town to give a retreat. It was my job to drive him to the retreat house after he had shared a meal with the novitiate community. Mind you, this is in a different city from where he lived, and it was also a part of town unfamiliar to me. I was given directions to the retreat house, but in the course of our talking along the way, I got lost because I wasn't paying attention. I panicked a bit, but when I indicated to the retreat director that I was lost, he just asked me to describe what I saw around there along the streets. I did so, and somehow he was able to guide me back on track to the retreat house. I still am not sure how he did that.

In his blindness, the retreat director had refined his other senses and abilities to move through life seemingly without missing a beat. But that's why a story he shared was so powerful. He described being on vacation in the woods in Wisconsin. One day he was out for a walk along a dirt path. Somehow along the way, he got turned around and didn't know which direction to go to return to the house. So once he found a paved road, he decided to just stand in the middle of the road and wait to be found by someone passing by.

Wait to be found. That phrase has echoed in me at varying times over the years after I heard that story told so vividly. Wait to be found—that is certainly not an appealing strategy when I feel lost or confused or am trying to figure out where I'm going. But I know it's good advice. In fact, I give it to others all the time, so it must be good! But it's awfully tough to practice. Again and again, God invites me to stay still, open, and receptive to how he wants to approach me and find me and call me home to true life and freedom.

Back to the disciples and the risen Jesus. In all the Resurrection scenes we have reflected upon, Jesus was consistent in both *telling* and *showing* the disciples that he was with them in the present and would remain with them in the future. He reminded them of who they were as his friends and members of his beloved community, as members of the family of God, beloved brothers and sisters and children of his Father. And he did more than just tell them in words. He showed them in deeds that he was alive, that he was with them, that he still knew their names and was continuing to call them to share in his mission. And finally, he gave them his Spirit.

The risen Jesus renewed, in a sense, his calling of the disciples after all the trauma of his Passion, Death, and Resurrection. The callings look similar in a way. He finds some of the disciples in situations where they seem to have gone back to what they were doing before. Some have gone fishing; others have started to go back home to just put the whole thing behind them. What else could they do? They still have to live and provide for themselves. They also go back to what is familiar and what they know best.

But things are also different now. I spoke of ways that
Jesus reached the disciples in their grief and desolation to
draw them out of themselves once again. The call continues
to come. The call comes now, in the time of the Resurrection,
just as it did at the very beginning. Jesus meets the disciples
in their ordinary circumstances. He finds Peter, James, and
John on the seashore. Perhaps he found Matthew collecting
taxes. He speaks to them by name and calls them from their
ordinary life to something extraordinary, and yet the renewed
call meets them exactly where they are, still in the ordinary
circumstances of their lives.

At the beginning of the Acts of the Apostles, there is yet
another description of a call to the disciples. Right after Jesus
gives his mandate to go and teach all nations, baptizing them
in the name of the Father and of the Son and of the Holy
Spirit, he ascends into the heavens, to the right hand of his
Father. And as the disciples are looking up to the heavens,
trying to see where Jesus had gone, their vision is interrupted
by two angels. The angels admonish them, "Men of Galilee,
why are you standing there looking at the sky?" (Acts 1:11).
The glimpse of the Ascension is important. They know where
Jesus is headed and where they are headed, ultimately. But
now that they know their true end, they will discover the next
steps not by gazing up into the heavens but in coming back to
earth and following the promptings of the Holy Spirit, which
are to be found in community with each other. Those same
disciples, Acts recounts, immediately head back to Jerusalem,
find their companions, enter into prayer with one another,
agree to share everything in common, and then begin their
ministry to others so that they too might know their true end
and be given the encouragement to become free from what

is hindering them. They live their lives in true freedom and in love, according to the purpose for which they were made.

The stories from scripture that give shape to the earliest dimensions of the life of the Church are meant to be gone back to again and again. Those stories are our stories as well. We can find ourselves within them. If we get disoriented by what life brings to us over the years, we can find our center again by looking to these stories. What constitutes this center is friendship with the very same Jesus of Nazareth, and the very same Holy Spirit prompts us toward greater freedom by remembering who we truly are, called by name as beloved daughters and sons of the very same Father. And we get reoriented in all these relationships and rediscover these true identities of who we are, not simply by thinking about these truths in our own heads, but by opening up our hearts and lives and actions to the world around us. We find our true selves by living lives of outward love, freedom, and joy in communion with those in our own corners of the world. So, let's begin again!

Exercises to Cultivate Habits of Freedom

1. Take some time and skim back over this short book. Is there anything you'd like to take away especially?
2. Come before God right now and feel him gaze upon you in love. What does he say to you? What does he want you to remember about your true identity?
3. Spend time considering what habits of freedom you want to start cultivating, both in words and in deeds. What habits will help you reject how the enemy causes you to cave in on yourself, and which habits might help you get back on track, living out of what God desires for you?

Acknowledgments

My sincere thanks to Judi Buncher and Virginia Herbers for accompanying me in the writing of this book. We participated in the instability of the pandemic and our shifting work lives together and I am most grateful for the companionship along the way. And special thanks to Judi for writing the small-group discussion guide for the book. No doubt small groups who use the book will benefit from her wisdom and prayerfulness. Finally, thanks to Fr. Casey Beaumier, SJ, and Fr. Bill Leahy, SJ, for the hospitality shown at Boston College during the sabbatical that made this book possible.

Small-Group
Discussion Guide

Whether you're reading *Habits of Freedom* with a group from your parish, in your regular small group or book club, or on your own, this guide is designed to help you get the most out of your reading. The questions are designed to be read and discussed after each chapter. If you're reading this on your own, take time after each chapter to pray and reflectively consider these questions. If you're reading this book as part of a group, instructions for the facilitator of the group are below.

Instructions for Facilitators

This study guide is designed to cover the five chapters and conclusion in one- to two-hour meetings, but this schedule can be adjusted to meet the needs of the group. If a group is being created specifically to discuss this book, you might find it helpful to have a half-hour introductory session in which group members can meet each other and books can be handed out prior to the first meeting for discussion.

When we come together as a group to share our experience of God and how he speaks to our hearts, the best gift we can give each other is the gift of being heard. We offer ourselves to each other by being present, listening, and embracing the grace that each person brings to the group. When someone shares, be comfortable in the pause, as members collect their thoughts before responding. This moment can lead to greater insight.

Materials Needed

- *Habits of Freedom: 5 Ignatian Tools for Clearing Your Mind and Resting Daily in the Lord*
- Journals for personal preparation and reflection before or after the group discussion

1. Allow Disruption

Opening Prayer

Lover of my soul, help me to recognize the consolation you give and the grace to move in the direction of greater faith, hope, and love. Help me to recognize and reject that which leads to desolation and leaves me in fear and anxiety. Lead me into freedom and greater love of you. In my time of confusion, indecision, and wandering, ground me in the knowledge of what you call me, beloved daughter/son of God. Help me to hold the vision of my baptism close at heart, and to hear your voice of love telling me who I am. Lord help me to see your presence in the uncertainties of life, when life is full of change and choices are not clear. Open my eyes to see your light in the darkness and hear your voice in my heart. Grant me faith to trust that you are intimately with me as I traverse the path I am on.

Reflection Questions

1. God led the people of Israel into the dessert where they had nothing and no one to rely on but God. They had to rely on him for every need. Have you had an experience of the desert? What was it like? Did you see new life emerge? How did you see God in the desert?

2. Hosea 11:3–4 speaks of God's tender care for his beloved, who "did not know that I cared for them." Have you had a child or loved one who was unaware of the loving care you gave to them until they needed you? What did that situation feel like?

3. Fr. Chris ultimately found freedom in the experience of moving states during his junior year of high school. He was involuntarily redirected and opened to a new world of choices. Has a redirection in your life caused a sense of freedom for you? What are some of the new choices that were available to you?

4. The Examen that St. Ignatius requires of his Jesuits is the act of looking at the moments of your day, the people, the places, the words . . . feeling the emotions again and recognizing God in it all. Have you ever had a memory surface in the quiet? Did you see it in a new way? Did it make you grateful? If so, how?

5. Fr. Chris talks about scripture and the way God speaks to us in his living Word. Can you share a scripture that has touched your heart at a time when you needed to hear God's voice?

Closing Prayer

Dear Jesus, in gratitude I come to you this day. May my heart be disposed and open to all that you have for me this day. May I reflect and see the events and people of this day in the light of your love. I ask for your peace, trusting you have created me to walk with you.

2. Remember Who I Am
and Whose I Am

Opening Prayer

Dear Jesus, as I wake each day help me to remember that I am yours and that you hold me in your heart in all the challenges and joys that come my way. You are with me; I am not alone. Help me to live in the present, letting go of the past and not speculating on the future. When I feel unworthy, may I turn to you in hope and trust, remembering my baptism, that I am yours and you love me as a father loves his own. Each day I ask, "A clean heart create for me, God; renew within me a steadfast spirit" (Ps 51:12).

Reflection Questions

1. In Genesis we hear that everything good was given to Adam and Eve to receive and enjoy. They are soon tempted to question and speculate, taking them out of the present conversation with God. What brings you out of the present moment and out of conversation with God?

2. Adam and Eve forget their true identity, their ability to see clearly leaves them. They fall for the lie of the enemy who insinuates that they lack something; it is then that fear and anxiety set in. What makes you forget your true identity?

3. God continues to remind his people the truth of who they are. He sends Abraham, Moses, and prophets with the message that they belong to him. How has God reminded you of who and whose you are? Who is your prophet?

4. Pope Benedict reminds us that from the moment of baptism, each person shares in the very same relationship that Jesus has with his Father. When you think of your baptism in this light, how do you feel about the Father? What does this say about his feelings toward you?

5. Names . . . we long to be called by name, to be known.
   Think of a time in your life when your name was spoken
   in love, in joy, in delight. Imagine God saying your name.
   What is the story of your name?

Closing Prayer

Father, I long to hear your voice. Whisper your loving words
to me; help me to hear and believe your Word that I am your
beloved.

3. Reject the Lie

Opening Prayer

Holy Spirit lead me in the way of faith, hope, and love. Give me a spirit of openness and freedom that takes me out of myself and into relationship with you and the people I meet each day. When the spirit of desolation tempts me, help me to let go of insecurity and turn to you in patience and trust until clarity returns. Jesus, be with me as I place my trust in you.

Reflection Questions

1. When important decisions present themselves, it is easy to turn in on oneself and become self-occupied with thoughts, doubts, and negative feelings. This can lead to desolation, and St. Ignatius says a decision should never be made in desolation. Can you think of a time in your life when a decision was postponed because the feeling wasn't right? Can you share?

2. In desolation I must just keep doing the next thing in front of me, rest in the discomfort, and be okay in the waiting. This is difficult. Have you had to do this, and what was the result?

3. Just as there are feelings that are stirred up in desolation, so it is in consolation. In consolation the Holy Spirit gifts a person with "courage, strength, consolations, inspirations, tears, and peace." Is there a decision that you felt consolation in? What were the feelings that came with that decision?

4. Jesus's source of strength was the confirmation (at baptism) that he was the beloved son. This gave him the strength to fulfill his mission of getting that message into each person's heart. How can you help Jesus get that message into the hearts of those you know and love?

5. God speaks eternally to us in the present tense. Do you
   find yourself caught in the past or the future? How do you
   think that effects your relationship with God?

Closing Prayer

Dear God, be with me as I try to live in the present moment
with you, remembering your living words to me: "You are my
beloved son/daughter in whom I am well pleased."

4. Talk It Out

Opening Prayer

Father, thank you for the relationships you have given to me. Lead me to the voices of wisdom in my life and draw me out of myself when I need a listening ear, or when someone else needs the voice of encouragement in their life. Bring me to your living Word and help me recognize your voice as spoken to me today.

Reflection Questions

1. We may sometimes be drawn into thinking about God and ideas about him, and forget that he loves us and wants a relationship. How do you listen and talk to God?

2. "Indeed, the word of God is living and effective, sharper than any two-edged sword" (Heb 4:12). The stories in the Bible are alive with dialog, two-way conversations, and action that can capture our imaginations. They are meant to draw us in, engage us, and bring us out again. Is there a particular Bible story that you can place yourself in? What questions would you ask? Tell us about it.

3. On the road to Emmaus the disciples were lost in conversation, and it wasn't the kind that was life giving. Rather, it was the kind of conversation that leads to isolation and discouragement. Jesus came on the road and talked with them as a friend. When your faith is tested by trial and Jesus seems far away, can you imagine him walking with you? What would he say to you?

4. As Jesus walked with the disciples on Emmaus, he asks, "What are you discussing as you walk along?" Jesus draws them into dialog and listens to them as they tell him all that has happened. Jesus offers patient listening before he speaks. Listening is a gift we give and receive. When has your listening been a gift to someone? When has someone's listening been a gift to you?

5. Jesus wants to hear our stories, and it helps us to tell them
    to him. Have you noticed a shift in your feelings or reac-
    tions when you have taken time to tell your stories to
    Jesus? Describe the difference.

Closing Prayer

Jesus, walk with me and open my ears to hear your response
to my stories. Holy Spirit, move within me so I may remember
and understand the words that God speaks to my heart.

5. Go on Offense

Opening Prayer

Dear Jesus, thank you for your words that remind me of whose I am, your words of encouragement and love. In remembering your desire for relationship with me, may I always take the time to converse with you about what is happening in my life. Help me to remember I am made for relationship with you and those you bring into my life. Guide me to move past my inertia to a life of action and openness to the experiences of you. May I begin to "see all things new in Christ."

Reflection Questions

1. Can you think of a time when an interruption became a moment of grace? How was your spirit as you went forth from the interruption?

2. Jesuits are called to find God in all moments of the day, not just in the "churchy" things they do, but also in the times when they are engaged in their regular works. How do you "see God in all things" in the work you do?

3. How has this time of isolation during the pandemic put you into a state of inertia? What can you put in motion to get out of yourself?

4. Do you have something in your life that causes you to be stuck? What change do you need to make? Is there something that the spirit is asking you to "fast" from so you can move forward?

5. Is there something in your heart that keeps resurfacing? Do you think Jesus is wanting to heal you? What do you think of the way that Jesus healed Peter's feelings of guilt?

Closing Prayer

Jesus, I thank you for my emotions. Help me to take notice and talk to you as a daughter or son who is beloved. Help me to hear your voice of love and affirmation, and grant me patience and wisdom.

Conclusion

Opening Prayer

Lover of my soul, help me to recognize the consolation that
you give and the grace to move in the direction of greater faith,
hope, and love. May I recognize and reject that which leads
to desolation and leaves me in fear and anxiety. Lead me into
freedom and greater love of you. In my time of confusion,
indecision, and wandering, ground me in the knowledge of
what you call me: beloved daughter (or son) of God. Help me
to hold the vision of my baptism, hear your voice of love, and
feel your embrace. Lord, help me to see your presence in the
uncertainties of life; when life is full of change and choices are
not clear, open my eyes to see your light in the darkness and
hear your voice in my heart. Grant me faith to trust that you
are intimately with me as I traverse the path I am on.

Reflection Questions

1. Jesus led the disciples out of their comfort zone and into
    many uncomfortable situations. In the most trying times
    he told them to "not be afraid." The disciples came to
    trust the one who called them by name. They knew who
    they were when in friendship with him. How does Jesus's
    friendship define who you are when you are in the midst
    of trials?

2. In the times when you are lost and confused and "waiting to be found," what do you do?

3. Jesus came to the disciples in many ways after his resurrection. He made sure they knew he was there, that they were his brothers and sisters in the family of God, and that they were still called to share his mission. He drew them out of themselves and gave them his spirit. Do you feel the call of Christ today? How?

4. The disciples after the resurrection all headed back to Jerusalem to be together, pray together, live in community with each other, and share this good news with others. What does your community look like, and how do they share the good news?

5. Share with the group an idea from this book or the group
    discussion that you will remember and come back to.

Closing Prayer

"Take, Lord, and receive all my liberty, my memory, my understanding, my entire will—all that I have and call my own. You
have given it all to me. To you, Lord, I return it. Everything is
yours: do with it what you will. Give me only your love and
your grace. That is enough for me."

—St. Ignatius of Loyola

Fr. Christopher Collins, SJ, is the vice president for mission at the University of St. Thomas in Minnesota. His research and teaching have been in the areas of systematic theology and spirituality.

Collins is the author of *Three Moments of the Day* and *The Word Made Love*. He regularly gives retreats around the country based on the Spiritual Exercises of St. Ignatius of Loyola.

ALSO BY
CHRISTOPHER S. COLLINS, SJ

Three Moments of the Day
Praying with the Heart of Jesus

In the tradition of Michael Gaitley's bestselling
33 Days to Morning Glory, Three Moments of the Day
presents a classic Catholic tradition in a way that is fresh
and compelling. Christopher Collins introduces three simple,
yet powerful prayer habits that are at the foundation
of both the Sacred Heart devotion and Ignatian spirituality
and that assist the reader in turning intentionally
toward the Sacred Heart of Christ.

In *Three Moments of the Day,* Collins guides readers
through the morning offering, evening reflection,
and how to ponder the gift of the Eucharist throughout the day.

Using these foundational practices, readers will strengthen
their interior sensitivity of God's invitation to peace, resilience,
and healthy attachments. With Christopher S. Collins as your
guide, start your journey toward clearing your mind and resting
in the Lord ever anew with each day's arrival.

"A dynamic and entertaining invitation to the Church."
—Deacon James Keating
Director of Theological Formation Institute for Priestly Formation
Creighton University, Omaha, NE